Duden

Abiwissen

Englisch

Landeskunde

Dudenverlag
Mannheim · Leipzig · Wien · Zürich

Bibliografische Information der Deutschen Nationalbibliothek
Die Deutsche Nationalbibliothek verzeichnet diese Publikation in der Deutschen Nationalbibliografie; detaillierte bibliografische Daten sind im Internet über http://dnb.ddb.de abrufbar.

D C B A

Redaktionelle Leitung: Simone Senk
Redaktion: Linda Strehl
Autor: Ulrich Bauer

Herstellung: Andreas Preising
Layout: Horst Bachmann
Umschlaggestaltung: Hemm-communication.design, Filderstadt
Satz: Kösel, Krugzell
Druck und Bindung: Heenemann GmbH & Co., Berlin
Printed in Germany

ISBN 978-3-411-73881-6

1 Great Britain: Political Life and Political System

The **United Kingdom of Great Britain and Northern Ireland** – often called Great Britain or Britain – consist of four parts: England, Wales, Scotland and Northern Ireland.

Traditionally, the United Kingdom (UK) used to be a **unitary state** where political power lies with the central government at Westminster. Since the 1990s there have been a number of changes: Parliament decided to give a certain degree of autonomy to national assemblies in Scotland, Wales and Northern Ireland, a process which is called devolution.

The United Kingdom's system of government is known as the **Westminster system.** It consists of a constitutional monarchy in which

- the **Monarch** is head of state and
- the **Prime Minister** is the head of government.

Executive power lies with the UK government and the devolved governments of Scotland and Wales and the Executive of Northern Ireland.

Legislative power is exercised by the central government at Westminster and the two chambers of parliament, the **House of Commons** and the **House of Lords,** as well as by the Welsh and Northern Ireland assemblies and the Scottish parliament.

The **Judiciary** is independent of the executive and the legislature; there is no supreme court like in the United States.

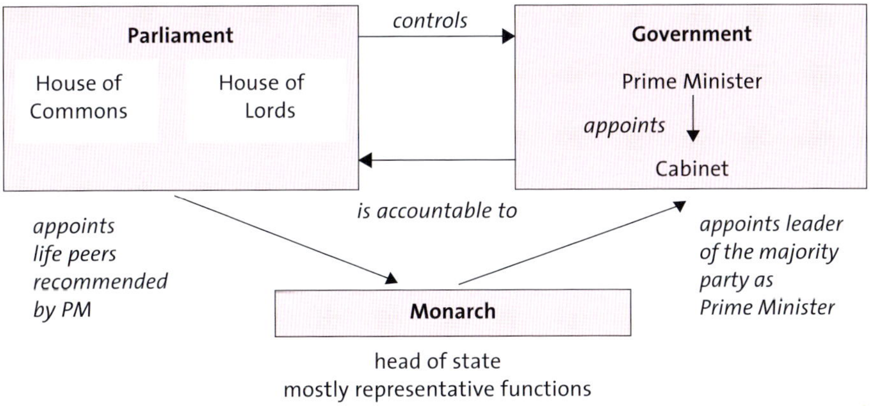

Great Britain's political system

Though Britain is a **constitutional monarchy,** there is no single document comparable to the Constitution of the United States. Instead, the constitution of the UK is the set of laws and principles under which the United Kingdom is governed.

Although the United Kingdom is – strictly speaking – a multi-party system, it is often seen as the classic example of a **two-party system.** This is because the two big parties – the **Conservative Party** and the **Labour Party** – dominate the political system due to the **First-Past-The-Post electoral system** used in general elections. Normally, this system ensures that one of the two big parties can form a government.

1.1 The British constitution

Most countries have a written constitution laid down in a single document like the Constitution of the US or the Grundgesetz in Germany. This is not true for Britain.

Basics **Constitution**

The constitution of a country is usually a written document containing all the important principles and rules governing the affairs of a nation. A constitution will typically establish the structure, procedures, powers and duties of a government and will also guarantee human rights.

It is sometimes said that Britain has an "unwritten" constitution. Although the constitution has indeed unwritten sources ("conventions"), most of it is in fact laid down in written form.

Basics **Sources of the British constitution**

1. **Acts of Parliament** – laws or statutes – that have received the approval of Parliament are among the most important sources of the constitution. These include historical treaties sometimes going back as far as the Middle Ages. **Magna Carta (1215)** or the **Bill of Rights (1689)** are two well-known examples. Parliament is considered by many to have the power to legislate on any subject it wishes.
2. **International treaties** that have been incorporated into domestic law by means of Acts of Parliament. One well known example is the European Convention on Human Rights which was incorporated into domestic law through the Human Rights Act 1998.
3. **EU law** has effect in the United Kingdom. According to some it can only become law in Britain if Parliament permits it to have effect, according to others Parliament has no choice but to permit it to have effect.
4. **Common law** where court judgements of the higher courts form precedents or case law that binds lower courts and judges.

Until recently, one thing was missing from the constitution: a document stating the rights of the citizens. This was rectified with the adoption of the European Convention on Human Rights, when specific rights that were not provided for in UK law were enacted in the Human Rights Act in 1998.

There is an ongoing debate whether the fact that Britain has no constitution like most other countries is an advantage or a disadvantage:

- **Advantage:** some contend that this gives the UK an unmatched flexibility in constitutional matters, making it easy to bring about political and social change.
- **Disadvantage:** others say that this can easily lead to a situation where important changes could be made without popular support. They argue that every citizen should know exactly what his rights are and that only a written constitution will make that possible.

1.2 Parliament

Britain is one of the oldest **parliamentary democracies** in the world and has become a model for many other countries. British parliament has been called "the mother of parliaments" because the system of parliamentary government was first developed in England.

Basics **Parliamentary democracy**

A parliamentary democracy is a system of government where parliament is at the centre of political power. It has the right to legislate, to elect the Prime Minister (not in the UK) and to control and overthrow the Prime Minister and his government.

The first English Parliament was formed in the 13th century. Over the following centuries Parliament slowly developed from a council to the Sovereign to a representative body effectively limiting the functions of the monarch, assuming ultimate power and establishing parliamentary sovereignty. Today the Parliament of the United Kingdom of Great Britain and Northern Ireland is the supreme legislative body in the UK. It has full law-making and executive powers and is neither controlled by a written constitution nor a Supreme Court like in the USA. Parliament is **bicameral,** consisting of an upper house, the **House of Lords,** and a lower house, the **House of Commons.** The two houses meet in different chambers in the Palace of Westminster, which is also known as the "Houses of Parliament".

1.2.1 House of Commons

The House of Commons consists of **646 Members of Parliament** (MPs). Each MP is chosen by a single constituency according to the First-Past-The-Post electoral system (see page 12), where only one of the candidates can win the constituency seat and where one vote more than the nearest rival is enough to win. MPs are elected for a five-year term. There are 529 constituencies in England, 40 in Wales, 59 in Scotland and 18 in Northern Ireland.

Main functions of the House of Commons:

- control of the government
- control of the state finances by approving budgets
- discussion of bills
- passing of bills into law (Acts of Parliament)

Although the Prime Minister is not elected by the House of Commons but appointed by the Queen, the British Government is answerable to the House of Commons. As a rule, the Prime Minister and most of his cabinet ministers are members of the House of Commons. Nevertheless it is questionable **who controls whom.** Although MPs have the power of passing a vote of no confidence, thereby bringing down the government, many critics argue that it is the Prime Minister and his Cabinet of ministers that have Parliament under control. Most important political decisions do not originate in Parliament but in the Cabinet.

The government uses the so-called "whips" to make sure that the government MPs follow the political line of the Prime Minister and his cabinet. Since it is in the interest of the MPs of the ruling party to keep the government in power and not risk defeating the government and lose their seat in a possible general election, it can be said that the Cabinet controls Parliament.

If the MPs of the ruling party are really dissatisfied with the Prime Minister and his politics, they will not normally defeat him in Parliament but try to bring about his fall by different means. For example, the pressure on Tony Blair got so strong in his third term as Prime Minister that he agreed to step down and make way for his successor.

Basics **Seating plan of the House of Commons**

- The way MPs are seated reflects the **two party system** in Britain. There are benches on two sides of the chamber, divided by a centre aisle. The Prime Minister and the Cabinet occupy the front bench on one side. On the other side there are the Leader of the Opposition and his Shadow Cabinet. In the centre aisle is the Speaker of the House who acts as a presiding officer. Members of Parliament who are neither members of the Cabinet nor the Shadow Cabinet have their seats on the back benches and are therefore called "backbenchers".
- The seating plan also reflects the **true division of political powers** in the UK: it is not Parliament as a whole that controls the government but it is just the opposition which attempts to control the government.

1.2.2 House of Lords

Functions

The House of Lords is the upper chamber in Britain's bicameral system. "Upper" is not to be confused with "more important". The House of Lords is far less powerful than the House of Commons. After a number of parliamentary reforms the House of Lords has been reduced to its judiciary role as **Britain's highest Court of Appeal** (The Law Lords) and its role as an institution which examines bills passed by the House of Commons and often suggests modifications to those bills. In theory the Lords can delay legislation up to a year. However, this does not happen very often, and for a good reason. Were the Lords to exercise this right too often, their political power would probably be reduced to zero by the government.

Members

The House of Lords has about 746 members. None of them are elected in any way. Its members mainly consist of two groups: **hereditary and life peers.** There are also two archbishops and 24 other senior bishops from the Church of England and 20 Law Lords who make up the final Court of Appeal. The largest group by far is the life peers, men and women who have been appointed members of the House of Lords by the Queen on the advice of the Prime Minister. The number of hereditary peers has been drastically reduced to just 92 (from over 750). Life peers rank as barons or baronesses and get their life peerage because of outstanding achievements in their fields, i. e. the arts, the sciences, literature, public service and so on.

Discussion **Should the House of Lords be abolished?**

Many people consider the Lords an anachronism in a democratic society where political leaders are elected by the voters, and for a limited time only. So why should there be an institution – as part of Parliament – nobody was elected to?

- People **in favour** of the continued existence of the House of Lords argue that debates in the House of Lords often have a higher intellectual quality than in the House of Commons. This is partly because party discipline doesn't play such an important role among the Lords; they can speak freely and openly and are less partisan than MPs. Another argument is that some of the brightest minds of the country often sit in the House of Lords, although there is no guarantee for that.
- People who are **against** the House of Lords in its present form argue that its members should either be elected or it should be abolished. They also see the House of Lords as a remnant of class society and argue that it has no real political function any longer.

There are a number of suggestions about the future of the House of Lords. The one with the biggest following seems to favour a fully elected Senate to replace the House of Lords. No practical political steps have been taken so far, however.

1.3 Political parties and the electoral system

Two big and one smaller party dominate Britain's politics:
- the Labour Party,
- the Conservative Party and
- the Liberal Democratic Party.

Most MPs belong to one of these parties. But there are a number of smaller parties with MPs, mainly the nationalist parties (Scotland, Wales and Northern Ireland).

Britain has traditionally been a country with a **two-party-system.** For many decades the two major parties – Labour and the Conservatives – have dominated British politics. Since the electoral system with its "the winner takes all"-system puts smaller parties at a disadvantage, the influence of these parties has always been rather limited. Coalition governments are rare; normally one of the two major parties is in government with the other major party taking over the role of "her majesty's opposition".

1.3.1 The Labour Party

History

The Labour Party was founded at the beginning of the 20th century. In the 1920s it took over the role of main opposition party to the Conservatives from the Liberal Party. Between 1924 and today (2009) the Labour Party was in government seven times. The Labour Prime Ministers were R. MacDonald in the 1920s, C. Attlee in the 1940s, H. Wilson in the 1960s and 1970s, J. Callaghan in the 1970s and Tony Blair from 1997 on. In 2007 Gordon Brown took over as Labour leader and Prime Minister from Tony Blair, who by that time was the longest serving Labour PM in history.

Political ideas

The Labour Party grew out of the trade union movement and socialist political parties of the 19th century, and continues to describe itself as a party of democratic socialism. The main aim has always been to look after the **interests of the poorer and less privileged people in society.** Traditionally, the party was in favour of socialist policies such as public ownership of key industries, government intervention in the economy, redistribution of wealth, increased rights for workers and trade unions, and a belief in the welfare state and publicly funded healthcare and education.

New Labour

Since the mid-1980s the party has moved away from its traditional socialist position towards a more **market-oriented position.** This was mainly initiated by Tony Blair, who was elected party leader in 1994 and called his re-orientation of the Labour Party both "New Labour" and the "Third Way".

Important political changes include an emphasis on individual responsibility and private initiative as opposed to the more traditional view of the state as some sort of protective agency providing for everything through welfare payments and general state intervention. Economically speaking Blair's reforms proved to be successful. In the late 1990s and the first decade of the 21st century the UK prospered economically, with good economic growth rates, low inflation and high employment. Other political changes included devolution for Wales and Scotland and strengthening Britain's role in the EU and the world.

1.3.2 The Conservative Party

The Conservative and Unionist Party is also known as the Conservative or the Tory Party. It was founded in its present form in the early 19th century. The Conservatives have traditionally been **the principal party of the political right or centre-right.** Their voters tend to come from the upper and middle classes, especially in the south of England with its modern high-tech and service industries. Apart from being Britain's oldest political party the Conservatives are also the most successful. No other party has had more election victories. Well-known Conservative Prime Ministers were Winston Churchill, Edward Heath and Margaret Thatcher.

After the Conservatives' defeat in the 1997 general elections and the three consecutive Labour governments the Tories have focused on different political issues like the environment, the improvement of government services like health care and education. This is especially true since David Cameron became the party leader. The Conservative party is still very sceptical towards the European Union and has strongly opposed the European single currency.

Biography **Margaret Thatcher (*1925)**

In 1979 **Margaret Thatcher** – "the Iron Lady" – became Britain's first female Prime Minister. Her government was characterized by a number of changes to the UK's economic and social system. As a convinced advocate of neo-liberal ideas Thatcher cut down the influence of the trade unions, reduced many social services and privatized formerly nationalised industries. She is also known for her uncompromising stand in the Falklands conflict with Argentina. She resigned in 1990.

1.3.3 The Liberal Democrats

The Liberal Democrats (or Lib Dems) were formed in 1988 by merging the traditional Liberal Party or Whigs with the Social Democratic Party, a splinter group from the Labour Party. The Liberal Democrats stand for more civil liberties, better social services, greater autonomy of Scotland, Wales and Northern Ireland and Britain's EU membership. Although they get a sizeable proportion of the popular vote in general elections, the electoral system prevents the Lib Dems from winning many seats in the House of Commons.

1

1.3.4
The electoral system

Winner Takes All

In general elections Britain uses the **First-Past-The-Post** (Winner-Takes-All) **system or majority vote.** The 646 Members in the House of Commons are all elected in one of 646 constituencies. The candidate who gets the most votes in a constituency is elected. Even the smallest possible majority is enough to win the seat. The votes for the other candidates in the constituency are "lost votes". Unlike the system of proportional representation, which makes sure that smaller parties also get seats in proportion to the total of the votes, these votes count nothing as far as winning a seat in Parliament is concerned.

An MP is elected for a five-year term. Since it is the Prime Minister's privilege to call a general election whenever he and his party think the time is right, MPs often serve shorter terms. On the average, general elections take place about every four years.

Unfair or effective?

The electoral system of majority vote or direct representation is considered by many to be unfair to smaller parties and to result in a distorted picture. In the 2005 general elections Labour got 35.3 %, the Conservatives 32.3 % and the Liberal Democrats 22.1 % of the popular vote, i. e. all votes cast. This translates into 356 seats for Labour, 198 seats for the Conservatives and 62 seats for the Liberal Democrats. Although there is only a gap of 3 % between Labour and the Conservatives as far as the popular vote is concerned, the gap between the number of MPs is enormous in comparison. The situation is even worse for the Liberal Democrats: their 22.1 % (almost six million votes) translate to just 62 seats in the House of Commons and reduce them to the status of a minority party in Parliament.

Discussion **Arguments for and against majority vote**

Pros:

- No need for coalition governments because normally there is a clear majority for one party: there will nearly always be a working government as a result of the election.
- Extreme right- or left-wing parties have almost no chance to win a seat in Parliament.
- Change of governments happens quite frequently and easily.

Cons:

- The system is very unfair to smaller parties. They might have considerable popular support but still win very few or no seats at all.
- The system does not reflect the overall political leanings of the voters.
- A party can win a majority of seats in the House of Commons without winning the majority of the popular vote. This can happen if one party has many very narrow victories in many constituencies (less lost votes) while the other party wins its constituencies with huge majorities ("unnecessary" majorities).

Supporters of the system of majority vote point out that the system is effective inso far as it ensures a working majority for the winning party. The fact that Labour got almost twice as many seats as the Conservatives in 2005 shows that this is normally true. Under a system of proportional representation like the one used in general elections in Germany, the British 2005 result would have translated in a relatively small majority of seats for Labour, a very strong Conservative party and more than twice the number of seats for the Liberal Democrats. It would also have meant that no party could form a government alone.

1.4 Government

Her Majesty's Government consists of the **Prime Minister** and his/her **Cabinet.** By convention it is the leader of the party that has a majority of seats in the House of Commons who becomes Prime Minister.

1.4.1 The Prime Minister

As the name suggests, the "first" minister originally was meant to be first among equals, some sort of cabinet chairman. This has changed considerably over the centuries. Today the Prime Minister occupies a very strong position in the system of government in the UK and is, in fact, at the centre of power.

Basics **The Prime Minister's most important functions**

- He is the leader of the government.
- He is the de facto Commander-in-Chief of the British Armed Forces (although officially this position is held by the Sovereign).
- He chooses and dismisses Cabinet members.
- He advises the Queen and keeps her informed on state matters.
- He can decide the date of general elections by requesting the Queen to dissolve Parliament and to call a general election within the allowed framework of the five-year parliamentary term.
- He recommends appointments to the Queen such as archbishops, university posts and civil honours. This also includes peerages and knighthoods.

1.4.2 The cabinet

Senior ministers

The Cabinet is composed of about 20 senior government ministers chosen by the Prime Minister. Most members are head of government departments with the title of "Secretary of State" or "Minister". Usually all members of the Cabinet are MPs. In rare cases politicians not having a seat in the House of Commons have been members of the Cabinet.

Collective responsibility

Since the members of the Cabinet usually are members of Parliament they are accountable to it. This has led to the principle of **collective cabinet responsibility.** Collective cabinet responsibility means that members of the cabinet make decisions collectively, and are therefore responsible for the consequences of these decisions collectively. When a vote of no confidence is passed in Parliament, every cabinet member who holds a seat in the House of Commons is expected to resign from the executive. Collective responsibility also means that a member of the cabinet who does not agree with major government decision is expected to resign. In 2003, when Foreign Secretary Robin Cook did not agree with Tony Blair's decision to engage in the Iraq War, he resigned.

1.5 The sovereign

Constitutional monarchy

Great Britain is a hereditary **constitutional monarchy.** This means that the powers of the monarch are limited by the constitution. While formally and symbolically the powers of the Crown remain very great, the political reality is different. **"The Queen reigns, but she does not govern"** sums up the monarch's political standing today. On the whole, the Queen must follow the advice of government ministers.

Rights of the monarch

According to the constitutional writer Walter Bagehot the monarch has **three rights:** the right to be **consulted,** the right to **advise** and the right to **warn.** As a consequence of these ideals, Prime Ministers hold weekly confidential meetings with the monarch in which the sovereign holds the right to express her opinions.

Basics **Royal powers**

Whatever royal powers remain in practise are called **royal prerogatives.** These prerogatives are exercised by the **Prime Minster and the Cabinet** with the formal consent of the Queen. The most important are to:

- appoint the Prime Minster,
- dissolve and call Parliament,
- declare war,
- make international treaties,
- issue passports,
- approve bills ("Royal Assent"),
- create peerages and to grant knighthoods,
- give the "Speech from the Throne" in the House of Lords at the opening of a new parliamentary session (a speech written by the Prime Minister outlining the government's agenda).

Ceremonial role

As head of state, the monarch is known as the sovereign, although strictly speaking this is no longer true. Sovereignty in the UK no longer rests with the monarch. Instead the principle of Parliamentary sovereignty was established at the close of the 17th century. Today the sovereign has an essentially **ceremonial role.** In formal terms, the "Crown-in-Parliament" is sovereign even though in practical terms the political head of the UK is the Prime Minister. However, the real powers of position of the monarch in the British Constitution should not be downplayed. The monarch does indeed keep some power, but it has to be used with discretion.

Polls in Britain show that support for the monarchy is still strong. This is especially true for the Queen, who is very popular among her subjects. Although there is a movement in Britain advocating the abolishment of the monarchy and replacing it with a republican system of government, support is not very strong. There is, however, increased criticism of some members of the Royal Family as far as their life styles and personal relationships are concerned.

Discussion **Arguments for and against the monarchy**

Pros:

- Constitutional monarchy is well-established in Britain and has a long tradition.
- A monarch is better suited as head of state than an elected president because he / she is above (party) politics.
- The monarchy is also a tourist attraction which earns Britain significant income from visitors.

Cons:

- The monarchy is undemocratic because nobody elects the monarch.
- A monarch costs more public money than an elected president.

1.6 Devolution

Centralisation versus decentralisation

Before all political power was centralized in London, England, Scotland, Wales and Northern Ireland enjoyed a certain degree of independence. This all changed when central government got stronger and stronger from the 17th century onwards. For centuries the four countries played only a minor part in British politics. At the end of the 20th century, however, there were strong tendencies to change this and give Scotland, Wales and Northern Ireland more powers to make their **own decisions** and pass their **own laws.**

Reform

In the 1990s Parliament decided to give a certain degree of autonomy to **national assemblies** in Scotland, Wales and Northern Ireland. This process is called **devolu-**

tion and is defined as the "handing down" of powers from central government to government at regional or local level. To set up the new national assemblies local elections were held in 1999, which resulted in

- a Scottish Parliament,
- a National Assembly for Wales and
- a new Northern Ireland Assembly.

These assemblies now have the power to raise taxes or – in Scotland – to make all decisions concerning the country's educational system. **Decisive powers,** however, **remain with the central government** in Westminster (foreign policy, defence, monetary policy etc.).

Nationalism

In the Scottish Parliament election of 2007 the Scottish Nationalist Party (SNP) beat Labour to become the strongest party. In the elections for the Welsh National Assembly of the same year Plaid Cymru (The Party of Wales) was runner-up to Labour. These two results show the increasing importance of Scottish and Welsh nationalism over the past years. The constitutional status of Scotland is especially subject to ongoing debate. There are even plans for a referendum on Scottish independence from the UK.

2
USA: Political Life and Political System

The United States of America – also called the United States, the US, the USA or simply America – is a **federal constitutional republic** consisting of **50 states** and one federal district. **Basic documents** of US democracy are:

- the Declaration of Independence (1776),
- the Constitution (1787),
- the Bill of Rights (1791) and
- the writings of the Founding Fathers (18th century).

Typical of the US system of government is a specific form of the separation of political powers called **checks and balances.** The three branches of government – the legislative, the executive and the judicial – all have some authority to act on their own but are also controlled and regulated by the other branches.

- The **legislative branch** of the federal government is the United States **Congress;** it consists of the House of Representatives and the Senate.
- The **executive branch** consists of the **President** of the United States who is both head of state and government, as well as the military Commander-in-Chief.
- The **judicial branch** is headed by the **Supreme Court,** the highest court in the federal court system.

Two-party system

For most of its history the United States has operated under a two-party system. The two major parties are the **Democratic Party** ("center-left", "liberal") and the **Republican Party** ("center-right", "conservative"). While political parties usually dominate the political system in European countries, this is not true for the US: here political parties are little more than campaign organisations for the main elections.

Presidential elections

The most important elections on the national level are the Presidential elections which are held every four years. While Representatives and Senators are elected directly by the voters, the President is elected under a system of indirect election. The winner is determined by votes cast by electors of the United States Electoral College. This system has often been criticised as being outdated or even undemocratic.

2.1 The American Constitution

The United States Constitution is both the shortest and oldest written constitution of any major state. It was adopted and ratified in 1787 and consists of just seven original **articles,** a **preamble** and twenty-seven **amendments** (additions to the constitution). It is strongly influenced by the British system of government but also incorporates other political ideas of the Age of Enlightenment. The most important of these ideas are:

- the separation of political powers ("checks and balances")
- the separation of church and state
- the sovereignty of the people
- government by the people
- unalienable rights for every individual ("Bill of Rights")

We the People

Article. 1

Page one of the United States Constitution which was adopted on September 17, 1787 by the Constitutional Convention in Philadelphia, Pennsylvania.

In 1787, when representatives from the original thirteen states of the confederation gathered in Philadelphia (in a building known today as **Independence Hall**) in order to work out a constitution, there were two opposing groups: the **Federalists,** advocating a strong central government, and the **anti-Federalists,** arguing for strong individual states. A compromise was eventually found which allowed for a strong central government, but also gave the individual states a strong influence in the legislative branch of government by creating a legislature composed of two houses: the **Senate** and the **House of Representatives.** The Senate would represent the states (equal voting) and the House of Representatives would represent population (proportional representation).

The seven articles and the Bill of Rights

The seven articles of the Constitution cover the powers of **Congress,** the **presidency,** the powers and responsibilities of the **judiciary,** the relation between **states, amend-**

ments to the Constitution, the **authority** of the Constitution and the process of **ratification.**

In 1791 ten amendments were added to the Constitution. These **first ten amendments** became known as the **Bill of Rights,** which limit the authority of the government and guarantee the fundamental rights of all Americans. Important freedoms and rights guaranteed by the Bill of Rights are the freedom of religion, the freedom of speech, the freedom of the press, the freedom of assembly and the right to bear arms.

The right to bear arms

The right to bear arms, laid down in the Second Amendment ("the right of the People to keep and bear arms shall not be infringed"), is one of the most controversial and most contested rights today. It must be kept in mind that the right originated in the context of a militia, i.e. a people's army where citizens are expected to serve military duty and bear arms. Today courts in the US interpret the right to bear firearms in the context of individual self-defense within the home.

Discussion **Arguments for and against the right to bear firearms**

School shootings like the one at **Columbine High School** in Littleton, Colorado, in April 1999, where 15 people died, usually lead not only to widespread discussions about changes of schools' policies concerning discipline and security, but also about gun laws in general. The debate about **gun politics** has long been among the most controversial issues in American politics. This debate is basically about an individual's right to firearms under the Constitution and the duty of government to legislate gun laws to prevent crime and maintain order.

Pros for stricter gun control laws:
- The government must regulate guns.
- The Second Amendment to the Constitution is a *collective* right to own guns for communal defense only.
- Gun ownership leads to higher levels of crime.

Cons against stricter gun control laws:
- The government has no authority to regulate guns because gun possession is a fundamental civil right.
- The Second Amendment to the Constitution is an *individual* right to own guns.
- People should have the right to own and carry arms for self-defense.

2.2 The system of checks and balances

Through an effective system of checks and balances the US constitution makes sure that no one branch of government holds total power and each branch can be overruled by another:

- The powers of the presidency are undoubtedly great, but they are not unlimited: the Senate must approve most actions by the President.
- The President is free to choose the secretaries for his Cabinet, but the Senate must approve them.
- The President has no way to introduce bills (laws) in Congress and he has no "built-in" majority in either the House of Representatives or the Senate.
- The President has the right to veto any bill passed by Congress, which then can only become law if two-thirds of the members of both houses vote in favour of it.

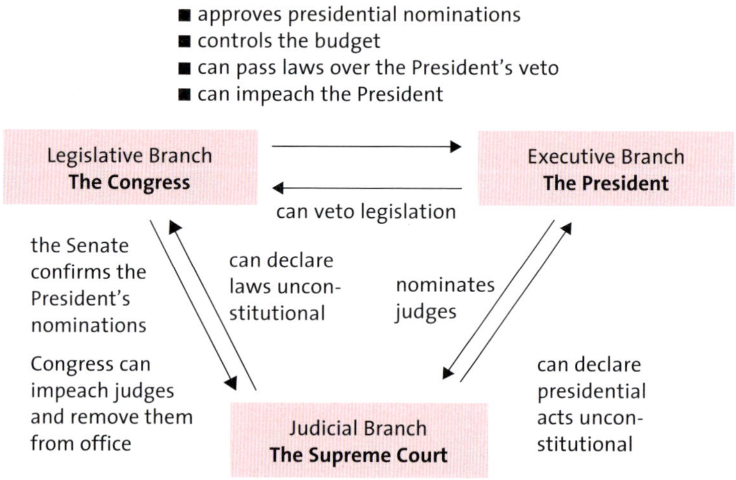

The system of checks and balances

2.3 The executive branch of government: the President

The US President is often called the most powerful man in the world. This is probably true as far as his military powers are concerned. Standing within the framework of the American **presidential democracy,** he is not quite as powerful as one might think, however. Although he is:

- head of state,
- head of government (Chief Executive) and
- **Commander-in-Chief** of the armed forces,

the President cannot "automatically" count on a majority in Congress like the British Prime Minister, who has a ("built-in") majority in the House of Commons and can normally be sure of its support. The American President can easily be in a situation where his own party has no majority in Congress. President Bill Clinton experienced such a situation when the Republican Party won a majority in both houses of Congress during Clinton's first presidency in 1994. In such a situation the President becomes potentially weak unless he manages to win the support of Congress by convincing enough senators and representatives to vote for his proposed measures.

2.3.1
Qualification and election

According to Article Two of the Constitution a presidential candidate must:

- be a natural-born citizen of the USA,
- be at least thirty-five years old,
- have been a permanent resident in the United States for at least fourteen years.

The President is elected every four years; no one can be elected President more than twice. The President is elected by the voters through the **Electoral College.** Under this system of **indirect election** each state has as many electors as it has Senators and Representatives in Congress. Strictly speaking the voters do not cast their votes for a presidential candidate on election day, but for electors chosen by the candidate's political party. It is these electors that select the President a couple of weeks after election day. A simple majority of 270 out of 538 electors is needed to be elected President.

2.3.2
The President's role in the system of checks and balances

As **chief executive** of the United States, the President is the head of the executive branch of government. He is elected by the voters – i.e. he has his own personal legitimation – and his office is separate from the legislature. This is typical for a **presidential democracy.** The President, therefore, is not responsible to Congress and cannot be removed from office by a simple vote of no confidence. This can only be done in a complicated procedure called **impeachment,** which involves both the Senate and the House of Representatives. On the other hand the President cannot dissolve Congress in the way a British Prime Minister can dissolve the House of Commons under the rules of a **parliamentary democracy.** Also, the President cannot directly introduce legislation since neither he nor the members of his Cabinet are members of Congress. He cannot even count upon the automatic support of Congress, even if his own party is in the majority. Often a President's political intentions may be considerably delayed by Congress. He can, however, **veto** any bill Congress passes. The veto can only be overruled by two-thirds of both houses of Congress.

2.3.3
Executive power: current issues

The modern presidency of the United States has been described as an **Imperial Presidency.** This term is used to describe a number of important changes that took place in the 20th century and led to the increasing power of the executive. It is argued that the US Presidency is out of control and exceeding its constitutional limits because the White House staff and an increasing number of advisory bodies (e.g. the National Security Council) are not controlled by and accountable to Congress.

This trend is magnified by the President's role in **foreign relations** and world politics. President Nixon, for example, acted without the consent of Congress when he continued the war in Indochina in the early 1970s.

Both the lengthy and complicated presidential **nomination system** and the **role of money** in the nomination process have been criticized. Only candidates that can come up with enough money to sell themselves in the media stand a chance of winning the nomination.

Basics **Arguments for and against the American presidential system**

A **presidential system of government** is characterized by an executive branch which exists separately from the legislature, to which it is not accountable and which cannot normally dismiss it. A **parliamentary system of government** is characterized by an executive branch which does not exist separately from the legislature, but is part of it. It is accountable to the legislature (parliament) and can be dismissed by it through a vote of no confidence.

Pros:
- The President is elected by the people and has a direct mandate.
- There is a clear and effective separation of powers.
- Potentially, there is more political stability, as the President has a fixed term and cannot be dismissed at any time like a prime minister.

Cons:
- There is a danger of the system becoming authoritarian, because the President has so much power.
- It is difficult to remove an unsuitable President from office before his or her term has expired.
- The system of checks and balances can lead to situations where the executive and the legislative branch block and blame each other.

2.4
The legislative branch of government: Congress

The legislative branch of government is **Congress.** It consists of two houses: the Senate and the House of Representatives.

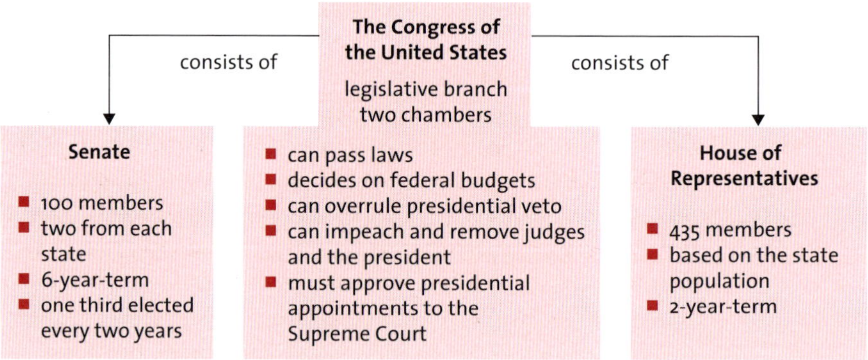

Congress: structure and main functions

2.4.1 The Senate

Under this **bicameral** system the **Senate** stands for equal representation of all the states. This is reflected by the fact that every state, regardless of its size and population, has two Senators. They are elected for a six-year term in state-wide elections. One third of the 100 Senators are elected every two years.

The **Vice-President** of the United States is the **President of the Senate.** He does, however, only attend important ceremonial functions, and it is only then that he actually presides over Senate debates. He can only vote to break a tie. Normally the President pro tempore (the most senior senator of the majority party) or a junior senator of the majority party presides over Senate debates.

Although the Senate and the House of Representatives are equal partners in the process of legislation (legislation cannot be enacted without the consent of both chambers), the Senate has some **unique powers:**

- It must consent to international treaties.
- It must agree to appointments of cabinet secretaries and federal judges.
- It has the sole power to actually try an impeachment case against a President (once the House of Representatives has decided to allow an impeachment).

2.4.2 The House of Representatives

Proportional representation

The **House of Representatives** stands for appointed proportional representation. Every one of its 435 members (often called "Representative", "Congressman", "Congresswoman") is elected for a two-year term in a congressional district representing on the average 700,000 persons. Therefore states with a relatively small size of population get less seats/Representatives than states with a much large population (e.g. Alaska 1, California 53). The presiding officer of the House is the **Speaker** who is elected by the members. There are also a Majority and Minority Leader.

Contrary to the Senate the House of Representatives has only few unique powers, among them the right to initiate spending bills and to impeach the President.

Legislative power

Article I of the Constitution gives all legislative power to Congress. It has authority over financial and budgetary matters and controls government spending. Its role in national defence includes the exclusive power to declare war and make rules for the military. Probably the most important non-legislative function of Congress is to control the government, i.e. the power to investigate and oversee the executive branch through congressional committees. Congress also has the exclusive **power of removal,** allowing the **impeachment** and removal of the President. So far only two Presidents have been impeached, Andrew Johnson in 1868 and Bill Clinton in 1999. In both cases the trials ended in acquittal.

Basics **The process of legislation**

Normally, proposed legislation is introduced in Congress as a **bill** by a member or members of either house. The President has no right to introduce a bill, he will have to find supporters among his own party and/or the other party to do this for him. Bills having to do with raising taxes may only be initiated by the House of Representatives.

Each bill goes through several stages in each house:

- presentation,
- committee (usually one of the permanent "standing committees"),
- hearing,
- approval of the committee,
- debate and approval of the house,
- debate and approval of the other house and
- submission of the bill to the President.

If the President approves of the legislation, he will sign the bill, thereby making it law. He may, however, choose to veto the bill and return it to Congress with his objections. Congress can only overrule the **presidential veto** with a two-thirds majority in each house. This leaves the President with the option of the so-called **"pocket veto":** he may choose to do nothing, neither signing nor vetoing the bill. In such a case, the bill automatically becomes laws after ten days. However, if Congress ends a legislative session during that ten-day period, then the bill does not become law.

2.5 The judicial branch of government: the Supreme Court

At the top of the federal judiciary is the Supreme Court of the United States. It is the highest judicial body in the US and consists of the **Chief Justice** and eight Associate Justices. All judges are **nominated** by the President and **confirmed** by the Senate. Presidents usually try to get people appointed to the Supreme Court who share their own political ideas. Justices are appointed for life, which makes them very influential in the long run.

The Supreme Court is mainly an **appellate court** which means that it reviews cases that are appealed to it from lower federal courts or the state supreme courts. Decisions are taken by a simple majority and are published in the form of majority decision and the dissenting opinion of the minority.

2.5.1 A policy-making body

The Supreme Court is not only the highest court of law. Within the system of checks and balances it uses the power of **judicial review** to assert its influence as a political institution. Although the Constitution does not explicitly grant the Supreme Court the power of judicial review, the Supreme Court has the well-established authority to **overturn laws and executive actions** it considers unlawful or unconstitutional. If the court exercises its power of judicial review, it guards and interprets the Constitution in a way similar to the German Bundesverfassungsgericht.

There has been an on-going debate about the **political role** of the Supreme Court. Some believe that judges are going beyond their powers and are making (instead of merely interpreting) the law; they are charging the judges of **judicial activism.** This is the antithesis to **judicial restraint,** a practice when the Supreme Court intentionally does not take up a political issue but leaves it to politics and politicians to find a solution.

Basics **Important Supreme Court decisions**

- Plessy vs. Ferguson (1886): the "separate but equal" doctrine makes racial segregation of public facilities legally possible.
- Wickard vs. Filburn (1942): the Court grants more powers to the Federal Government to make the New Deal possible.
- Brown vs. Board of Education (1954): segregation in schools unconstitutional.
- Roe vs. Wade (1973): abortion is a constitutional right.
- Regents of the University of California vs. Bakke (1978): affirmative action might be necessary to overcome discrimination.
- Furman vs. Georgia (1972): the implementation of the death penalty in many states is unconstitutional; the death penalty itself, however, is not unconstitutional.

2.6 Political parties

The US party system is quite different from the party systems in many European countries. For historical reasons there usually is a clear ideological division between the main political parties. In Britain, for example, the Labour Party traditionally was and to a large degree still is the party of the working classes, while the Conservatives stand for the interests of the middle and upper classes. Such a division has never existed among the two major political parties in the US. Generally speaking American political parties have **very little central ideology.** They are loosely organized, having **no formal organization** at the national level that controls membership, activities or policy positions. It is only for elections that American parties manage to find a common party line.

Basics **General characteristics of the American party system**

- The two major political parties do not represent particular social groups in society, but represent almost all groups of voters.
- Both parties are particularly strong in certain parts of the United States ("geographical" vote). While the Democrats have their strongholds in the Northeast, the Republicans dominate the West.
- There is no strong party loyalty among supporters and politicians. Since candidates for Congress can only become Senators or Representatives by winning their state or electoral district though majority vote, they are often more loyal to their voters than their parties. There is no party discipline like in Britain or Germany.
- The parties only become important every four years when they put up a candidate for the presidential elections.

2.6.1 The Republican Party

The Republican Party, also known as the **G.O.P** (Grand Old Party) was founded in 1854 by political groups that opposed the spread of slavery into the new territories. Its mascot is the elephant. It first came to power in 1860 when **Abraham Lincoln** was elected President.

The Republican Party is considered to be the more "conservative" of the two major parties. Republican Presidents include Herbert Hoover, Dwight D. Eisenhower, Richard Nixon, Ronald Reagan, George H. Bush and George W. Bush.

2.6.2 The Democratic Party

The Democratic Party is the older of the two major parties. It was founded in 1828 by political groups which were against a strong central government and favoured the autonomy of the states. Its mascot is the donkey.

The Democratic Party is considered to be the more "liberal" of the two major parties. Democratic Presidents include Franklin D. Roosevelt, John F. Kennedy, Bill Clinton and Barack Obama.

2.6.3 Other parties

Although the United States have in fact a two-party system, other parties exist on a national level. Except for the Republicans and the Democrats there are at least three other "third parties" that have a certain national importance: the Libertarian Party, the Constitution Party and the Green Party. But there is no doubt that the two major parties dominate American politics.

Today the **political stance** of the two parties differs in the following areas of politics:

	Democrats …	Republicans …
Fiscal policy/ taxes	… generally support a more **progressive tax structure** to provide more services and reduce injustice. They support more government spending on social services and welfare programs.	… tend to favour **tax cuts** for the wealthy as an incentive because they believe that reduced income tax rates will lead to more economic growth. They are critical of too much government spending on welfare programmes and are for limits on eligibility and benefits.
Health care	… favour **national health insurance** or universal health care to make sure that all Americans are covered.	… are against such an insurance scheme and favour a **personal or employer-based system** of insurance.
Environment	… believe that the government should protect the environment and that a sensible **energy policy** is very important.	… tend to believe that the market can provide better solutions to environmental problems than the state. They do not generally oppose state environmental programmes, however.
Social issues	… support **equal opportunity** and the expansion of civil rights. They are for affirmative action, stricter gun control and often oppose the death penalty.	… usually are against affirmative action, same-sex marriages and abortion. They support capital punishment and a firm stand against crime.
Foreign policy	… are against the doctrine of unilateralism, which states that the US should use military force without the assistance from other nations whenever it believes there is a threat to the country's security or welfare.	… advocate a strong national defense, interventionist foreign policy actions and unilateralism. Support for the war in Iraq is still strong among some Republicans.

Basics **The political spectrum of the two major parties**

While the political spectrum of European parties is often described in the context of "left" and "right", this context cannot really be applied to the US. In the 19th century, for example, the Democrats were considered the more conservative and the Republicans the more liberal party. This changed in the wake of the "Great Depression" in the first part of the 20th century. President Franklin D. Roosevelt's **New Deal** included the founding of Social Security as well as a number of other federal services and public works projects. This led to a polarization in national politics, turning the Democrats to the left and the Republicans further to the right.

Although both parties had liberal, moderate and conservative wings, in the 1960s the **conservative** wing became dominant in the Republican Party and the **liberal** wing became dominant in the Democratic Party.

2.7
Elections: the road to the White House

For a presidential candidate, the road to the White House is a lengthy and complex process. It starts well over a year before Election Day when a candidate officially declares that he/she is running for the presidency. This is when his **campaign** starts. A candidate will have to make great efforts to raise money for his campaign, build a campaign organization and make himself known to the voters through the use of the media and by travelling extensively.

autumn candidates declare themselves → **January–June** primaries and caucuses in some states → **summer** national party convention nomination → **November** election (indirect) → **December** electoral college elects president → **January** inauguration

The road to the White House

2.7.1
Primaries, caucuses and nomination

The candidate's aim is to be elected as a presidential candidate at **the National Convention** of his party in the summer before Election Day. To get there he will have to run in state **primaries** and **party conventions** or **caucuses.**

Primaries and caucuses take place in a number of states, starting in January of the election year and going on until the early summer. They give party members a chance to choose which candidates are to run in the presidential election. Successful candidates carry on until the summer, unsuccessful candidates drop out of the race during springtime. The year 2008 was unusual because Democratic candidate Hillary Clinton refused to accept defeat to Barack Obama until the very last moment, i.e. a few weeks before the National Convention.

The presidential candidate of each of the two major parties is chosen during the party's National Convention in August. Normally there is only one candidate left in the race and his **nomination** takes place in a well-staged show before thousands of delegates and the media. The candidate's "running mate" for the vice-presidency is also nominated on what is called a "ticket". The highlight of the nomination procedure is the candidate's **Nomination Acceptance Speech** which sums up the goals of his campaign and his political intentions if he is elected President.

2.7.2 Election and inauguration

Election day

Election day is on the Tuesday following the first Monday in November. This is when the voters cast their votes for **electors** chosen by the candidate's party. Due to the fact that the method of electing the American President is an **indirect** one, voters strictly speaking do not elect the President on Election day. They simply decide who of the candidates gets a majority among the members of the **Electoral College,** in which every state has as many electors as it has Senators and Representatives in Congress. The candidate who wins at least 270 (out of 538) electoral votes becomes President. If a candidate wins a majority of the popular vote in a state, he gets all the electors of that state.

During election night the important thing is which way the states go or **swing,** especially the states with a large population (and therefore many electors). When the "magic" number 270 flashes across the television screens, Americans and the rest of the world know who will be the next American President. The candidate is now the President-elect.

A couple of weeks after Election day the members of the **Electoral College** cast their votes. Although it is only now that the winning candidate is formally elected, this is a quiet and unspectacular affair that goes almost unnoticed by the public. Since electors are bound by the popular vote cast in November, electing the President is only a formality.

Inauguration

The winning candidate's road to the White House comes to an end on the steps of the Capitol in January of the following year when the new President is **sworn in** by the **Chief Justice** (the highest judge of the Supreme Court) and gives his **Inaugural Address,** a speech in which he outlines his policy.

3
Great Britain: Economy

The United Kingdom is one of the largest economies in the world. In Europe it is ranked second or third after Germany.

In the 18th and 19th centuries, the UK was the first country in the world to become industrialized. It is the "home" of the **Industrial Revolution** and played a predominant role in the global economy for most of the 19th century. Britain lost that role during the 20th century, due mostly to the war efforts of both World Wars and the end of the British Empire. However, it still has a significant role in the global economy and London is still one of the **financial centres** of the world.

3.1
Rise and decline

In the 19th century, Britain was the leading country in the world in terms of economy and trade. This **rise to a predominant position** had several reasons:

- Starting in the middle of the 18th century, Britain was transformed from a rural into an industrial country. **The Industrial Revolution** brought with it major changes in agriculture, manufacturing, mining, and transportation and had a profound effect on the socio-economic conditions in Britain. The textile industries were mechanized, iron-making techniques were improved, trade expansion was enabled by the introduction of canals, better roads and railways. Production capacity was increased through the use of steam power, water wheels and powered machinery.
- Britain had a **massive lead over other countries** in the process of industrialisation. This is often explained by the importance of natural or financial resources that Britain received from its many **overseas colonies** or profits from the British **slave trade** between Africa and the Caribbean. Others argue that Britain had a number of key resources: a dense population, natural resources (coal, iron, water) and a particularly effective agricultural system.

These factors – among others – lead to a rapid economic expansion with Britain taking the lead in manufacturing, trade, banking and investment of capital. The UK held this position up to the turn of the 20th century.

By the mid-20th century, Britain had lost its position as one of the leading industrial nations in the world. The period after 1945, especially the 1960s and 1970s, was characterized by **industrial decline and economic stagnation.** At times Britain was known as "the sick man of Europe" because of its low economic growth rates, its high rate of inflation, the devaluation of its national currency and the number of industrial strikes. The reasons behind this process were:

- the loss of colonial markets,
- the lack of innovation and modernization,
- low exports and increasing imports,
- conflicting economic policies alternating between nationalisation and privatisation,
- bad industrial relations between the Trade Unions and management and
- inadequate infrastructure (motorways, railways).

This situation started to change under the Government of **Margaret Thatcher** in the 1980s. Her economic policies (Thatcherism) brought about **fundamental economic change** in Britain.

Basics **Thatcherism**

Margaret Thatcher, who was Prime Minister from 1979 to 1990, was a staunch advocate of **neo-liberal ideas.** She believed in reduced state intervention, free markets, a reduction in the size of the Welfare State and entrepreneurialism – the freedom of private owners of enterprises in a capitalistic society. She also believed in **monetarism,** an economic theory which holds that the state must not intervene too much in the economy and that free-market economies are basically stable.

Her **reforms of the 1980s** included:

- reducing the influence of the Trade Unions,
- reductions in taxation to promote business,
- reductions in public spending, especially on welfare, and
- privatisation of formerly nationalised industries (e. g. railways, telecommunications).

Margaret Thatcher's premiership was marked by a lot of social unrest, industrial strife and high unemployment.

Critics of Thatcher's policies claim British society is still feeling the effect of her divisive economic policies and the culture of greed and selfishness they allegedly promoted.

Supporters of Thatcher claim that she has transformed Britain's stagnant economy and "tamed" the Trade Unions.

3.2 The situation since the 1990s

The 1990s saw a new **economic boom** and in recent years Britain has seen the longest period of sustained growth for more than 150 years. The British economy is one of the strongest EU economies in terms of inflation, interest rates, personal incomes and unemployment.

This ended in 2008 when the United Kingdom entered a recession brought about by the global financial crisis. The slowdown in growth is expected to put many businesses under substantial pressure.

Basics **The global financial crisis**

Britain – like almost every other country – was hit by the global financial crisis in 2008. Originally a **financial crisis,** caused by the mishandling of "bad debts" by many banks, the crisis not only affected banks and stock markets but turned into a **global economic crisis** seriously affecting production, trade and employment.

To fight the crisis, the British Government has nationalised banks and put billions into the economy in hope of reviving it.

4
USA: Economy

The economy of the United States is the **largest national economy** in the world with a gross domestic product (GDP) of over $ 14 trillion in 2008. It is a typical service economy with more than 78 % of the GDP generation in the services sector (agriculture: 1 %, industry: 20 %). America is a leader in technological advances, in computer and aerospace technology and in the development and production of medical and military equipment.

Due to the strength of the US economy Americans have a very high standard of living – it is among the highest in the world.

4.1
Rise to economic power

In 1776, when the American colonies became the United States of America, the economy was small, based on independent farming. By the end of the 19th century this economy had become **industrialized** and was one of the largest and strongest in the world. The main causes were:

- a large unified domestic market (due to the size and political unity of the country),
- vast areas of highly productive farmlands,
- vast natural resources (especially timber, coal and oil),
- an entrepreneurial spirit and a commitment to investing in material and human capital,
- the Protestant work ethic (wealth through hard work to please God),
- the frontier spirit (an attitude of inventiveness and self-reliance),
- a sprit of free enterprise,
- a constant supply of (cheap) labour through immigration and
- a high level of geographical, social and economic mobility.

4.2
The role of the government

The US economy is far from being an unregulated economy. There has always been a strong belief, however, that government should not interfere too much with the economy and should restrain from too many regulations.

For most of the 19th century the country had a **laissez-faire economy,** i. e. a **free market economy** free of government intervention and regulation, where decisions by businesses were based on the needs of the market.

This laissez-faire approach was restricted with the introduction of **anti-monopoly** and **anti-trust** laws that were meant to prevent monopolies such as electric companies from charging extremely high prices and to strengthen market forces so that direct regulation is unnecessary.

At the time of the **Great Depression** in the early 1930s, the government gave up its traditional policy of non-intervention and introduced a complex system to stabilize prices for agricultural goods, which tend to fluctuate wildly in response to rapidly changing supply and demand. A number of other industries – trucking and, later, airlines – successfully sought regulation, to limit what they considered as harmful price cutting. Laws to protect workers and standards of business practice were also introduced.

While regulation and state intervention is not unknown in the US, its economy is still less regulated in comparison with the economies of most European countries. One example is the lack of government interference with the problem of industrial pollution, where American governments still tend to leave it up to the individual companies to bring about improvements.

The **global crisis** of 2008/09 has left the Obama administration no choice but to step up state intervention to a so far unknown degree.

4.3 The US economy at the beginning of the 21st century

Since the turn of the century, the United States economy has moved from the era of industry into a **post-industrial era** and has become a **post-industrial economy.** The proportion of people employed in agriculture and manufacturing has decreased dramatically, while increasingly more people are employed in service-providing businesses.

Main economic sectors of the United States

- The USA is the world's leading manufacturer. **Main industries** are petroleum, steel, motor vehicles, aerospace, telecommunications, chemicals, electronics, food processing, consumer goods, lumber and mining.
- **Agriculture** is a major industry in the United States which is a net exporter of food. Top agricultural products are corn, cattle (meat), milk, chicken (meat), soybeans, pig (meat) and wheat. Between 2 and 3 % of the working population is employed in agriculture.
- The **service sector** (or service industries) with services like transportation, distribution and sale of goods, entertainment, telecommunication, banking, insurance, education and information generates more than three quarters of the US GDP and is by far the largest sector of the economy.

- The fastest growing sector within the service industry is what often is called the **quaternary sector,** i.e. mainly intellectual services: information generation, information sharing, consultation, education and research and development.

Apart from the numerous problems the US economy faces in the wake of the global crisis of 2008/09, its **main problems** are:

- a huge state deficit (public debt) of well over $ 10 trillion,
- external debt of over $ 13 trillion (money the US owes to other countries),
- a sizeable trade deficit,
- the costs of the "war on terrorism",
- a low savings rate and an extremely high rate of personal debt (credit financed consumerism),
- an increase in energy prices and
- uncompetitive industries (e. g. the car industry).

Despite of these problems, the US is still a world leader in many areas, computers being one of them.

Basics **Silicon Valley**

Silicon Valley is the southern part of the San Francisco Bay Area in Northern California. The term originally referred to the region's large number of silicon chip innovators and manufacturers, but eventually came to refer to all the high-tech businesses in the area; it is now generally used as a term for the **high-tech sector.** It was in Silicon Valley that the integrated circuit, the microprocessor, the microcomputer, among other key technologies, were developed. Silicon Valley has been the site of electronic innovation for over four decades, sustained by about a quarter of a million information technology workers.

Firms like Apple, AMD, Hewlett-Packard, Google, Intel, Nvidia, Yahoo and many others all have their headquarters in Silicon Valley. The valley is also home to a number of universities, amongst them Stanford University. Today Silicon Valley is one of the largest high-tech centres in the USA.

5
Great Britain: Education

There is no common educational system in the UK. Central government in London is only responsible for England, while Scotland, Wales and Northern Ireland have developed their own guidelines. The educational systems of the four countries have not drifted apart too much, however, and they still have many **common features.**

- State education in Britain is based on the **Butler Education Act of 1944.** It states that state education is **free and compulsory** from the age of five to the age of 16. There are plans to raise the age until which students must continue to receive some form of education or training to 18.
- State schools follow the **National Curriculum** which was introduced in 1988.
- Schooling is divided up into primary (ages 5–11) and secondary (ages 11–16) education.
- Most schools are **comprehensive schools** (similar to the German "Gesamtschule"); they are attended by children of all abilities (non-selective schools).
- Most pupils leave school with either the **GCSE** exam (General Certificate of Secondary Education) at the age of 16 or the **A-level** exams (Advanced Level) at the age of 18. A-level is required for university entrance.

5

Higher education consists of studying for a bachelor's degree at a university. Postgraduate students may decide to obtain a master's degree or a doctor's degree.

Private education is an import sector in education. Approximately 8 % of British children go to independent fee-charging schools, mainly prep schools (ages 7–13) and public schools (ages 13–18).

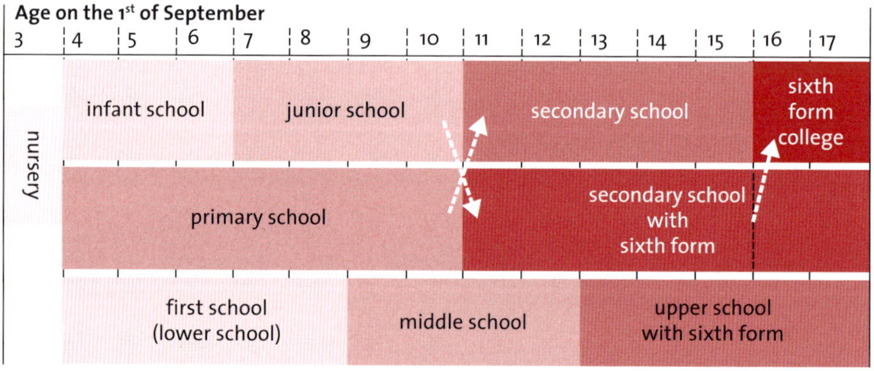

The most common patterns for schooling in the state sector

5.1 Schools

The British school system is a **dual system** consisting of **state** and **private schools.** Although only about 8 % of all pupils attend private fee-paying schools, the importance of the private educational sector should not be underestimated. More and more middle-class parents are sending their children to private schools because they believe that their children stand a better chance in life with a private education. They doubt the efficiency of comprehensive schools and are concerned about falling academic standards and a lack of resources at state schools. Many middle-class families therefore try at all costs to get their children in to one of the public schools. They are prepared to pay a lot of money for a public school education even if it puts a huge financial burden on them.

5.1.1 State schools

National Curriculum

All state schools in England, Wales and Northern Ireland must follow the National Curriculum which was introduced by the UK government in 1988. It does not apply to independent schools, which are free to set their own curriculum, as long as they are providing a reasonable standard of education. These are the main aims of the National Curriculum:

- The school curriculum should aim to provide opportunities for all pupils to learn and to achieve.
- The school curriculum should aim to promote pupils' spiritual, moral, social and cultural development and prepare all pupils for the opportunities, responsibilities and experiences of life.

Pupils are tested in all subjects at the key ages of seven, eleven, 14 and 16.

Basics **Core and foundation subjects in the National Curriculum**

Core and foundation subjects in the National Curriculum (2002):

- English
- mathematics
- science
- art & design
- citizenship
- design & technology
- geography
- history
- information & communication technology
- modern foreign languages
- music
- physical education

5

Primary education

In England, Wales and Scotland, compulsory education starts at the age of five. Children under this age can attend playgroups or nursery schools. **Primary schools** are usually co-educational schools for boys and girls where they teach general topics and put an emphasis on reading, writing and maths.

At the age of eleven – after six years in primary school – pupils are transferred to secondary schools.

Secondary education

Almost all children aged 11–16 attend **comprehensive schools.** Comprehensive schools came into existence in the 1960s as they are schools for students of mixed ability. One of the main ideas behind comprehensive schools was to prevent an early selection process which took place under the old system, when students had to take the "11-plus-exam" in their last year at primary school. The result of that exam decided which type of school a pupil could attend. The comprehensive school did away with that and made sure that all pupils attend one school between the ages of eleven and 16. This does not mean, however, that all students actually do and learn the same all the time. Comprehensive schools "stream" their students according to ability, i. e. put them in different groups.

Discussion **Arguments for and against comprehensive schools**

Pros:

- Comprehensive schools offer better opportunities to children, especially those from a working class background.
- They provide a diverse mixture of students from all classes and ethnic groups in society.
- They provide greater equality, especially by helping less talented students.

Cons:

- Academic standards are lower in most comprehensive schools.
- Comprehensive schools are often too big with up to a thousand students.
- There are social problems like vandalism and truancy in some inner city comprehensive schools.

There are still a number of **grammar schools** where pupils have to pass an entrance exam to attend. Grammar schools put an emphasis on academic subjects and prepare their pupils for a university education or for entry in to a profession. Other selective secondary schools are **secondary modern schools** (concentrating on vocational courses) and **technical schools** (concentrating on career-oriented subjects).

Basics **Examinations**

At the age of 16:
General Certificate of Secondary Education (GCSEs)
Most pupils take GCSEs in between six and nine subjects. English, maths and science are compulsory.

General National Vocational Qualification (GNVQs)
GNVQ is a more practical, vocational alternative to GCSEs, concentrating on practical work and problem solving.

Students who leave school at the age of 16 may continue their education at an evening institute, a technical college or a college of art.

At the age of 18:
General Certificate of Education Advanced Level (A-level)
After an extra two years of study students take their A-levels. Most students take three subjects, often maths plus two sciences or English plus two languages. Grades are from A (best) to E (worst). At least a B or C is usually required by universities.

Advanced Supplementary Level (AS-level)
This relatively new exam enables students to study a broader range of subjects. Since it takes only half the study time of A-level, it counts as half an A-level for university entrance qualifications.

5.1.2 Private education

Independent schools are attended by about 8 % of British children. There are about 2,500 independent schools in Britain. All of them charge fees. Schools fees average over € 20,000 for boarding pupils and over € 10,000 for day pupils. Extra money will have to be paid for uniform, equipment and facilities. It is obvious from these figures that only a small minority of parents can afford this. Some parents, however, make enormous sacrifices to send their children to these schools, and scholarships are offered to attract brighter pupils.

Independent schools are free to choose their own students, subject only to the general legislation against various forms of discrimination. Compared to state schools, independent schools nearly always have better teachers, longer teaching hours, more time for sports, extra-curricular activities and a much better pupil-teacher ratio. They also put a stronger emphasis on achievement, whether academic, sporting, musical, dramatic, artistic or otherwise. Educational achievement measured in examination results is also much better, giving their students a better start in higher education.

Prep schools
Preparatory schools "prepare" children aged 7–13 for the Common Entrance Examination, which all children who want to attend public schools have to take.

Public schools

Public schools are private schools for pupils aged 13 to 18. They have a long tradition – some of them date back many centuries – and have contributed notably to education in England with their emphasis on developing both the social and personal qualities of their pupils as well as their intellectual and academic faculties. Most of them still tend to be boys' schools.

The public schools have traditionally "produced" a large part of the British elite, with many of their pupils holding high office in government or other areas of public life. Among the best known public schools are Eton, Harrow, Winchester and Rugby.

Discussion **Arguments for and against public schools**

Pros:
- high academic standards
- better teachers
- smaller learning groups
- emphasis on social as well as academic skills

Cons:
- elitist
- old fashioned and traditionalist
- expensive; only relatively few parents (upper / middle class) can afford the fees
- arrogance and snobbishness

5

5.2 Higher education

Students who attend university usually do a three year course to get a **bachelor's degree (BA). Graduates** – i.e. students with a degree – can go on to take a **master's degree (MA),** and then do a **doctorate (PhD).** To qualify for a university course students normally need 3 A-level passes. Most universities base their decision to accept a student on both A-level grades and an interview.

There are approximately 200 universities in Britain. The **Oxbridge** universities (Oxford University and Cambridge University), which are amongst the world's oldest universities, are generally considered to be at the top or near the top of all UK universities. Most students go to the so-called **"redbrick"** universities situated in the major cities (London, Birmingham, Manchester, Bristol etc.). Most of them were founded in the 19th and 20th century and get their name as a lot of the university buildings were built from red brick. Many new universities were established in the second half of the last century, a lot of them on **campuses** in or close to smaller cities like York or Canterbury.

Basics The Open University

The Open University was founded in 1971 and it caters for people without the necessary A-levels for university entrance. **There are no academic prerequisites for enrolment.** The Open University is "open" to anyone and extends educational opportunities to all.

It is a non-residential university and provides study by means of **correspondence courses** and radio and TV programmes. Students study at home in their free time and only meet other students and their tutors once or twice per term.

5.3 Special features and problems

- The school year is divided up into **three terms** – autumn, winter, spring.
- English schools are **all-day schools.** Lessons usually run from 9–12 and 2–4. School meals are provided at lunch time.
- A majority of schools still require their pupils to wear a **school uniform.**
- School often begins with **assembly,** with all students and staff present. Assembly often starts with a religious part and is followed by announcements for the day.
- Extra-curricular activities like drama, music, debating, sports or clubs are an important part of school life.
- Social skills and a sense of community are considered important in all schools. This is reflected by community schemes: pupils look after elderly people etc.

Up to the 1970s, the major division in the British school system was between supporters of grammar schools and comprehensive schools. This conflict was resolved with the almost complete abolition of grammar schools in favour of a more egalitarian system. The division now runs between state schools and fee-paying private schools. The Labour government put a strong emphasis on education when it came to power in 1997 and put into effect a number of important **changes,** e.g.

- the creation of specialist schools with additional subjects like business studies,
- a scheme to identify high performing schools,
- the creation of Education Action Zones with the aim of improving schools in deprived areas,
- the provision of better services for children, young people and families and
- plans to extend the school leaving age in England to 18.

Despite all of these changes, a number of **problems** remain. The most important being:

- high truancy rates in some schools (pupils do not turn up for school),
- increasing aggression and violence in some schools which has led to an increase in security measures and
- a widening gap in school results of children from different social and ethnic backgrounds.

6
USA: Education

The United States' school system is totally **decentralized.** There is no national curriculum like in England and the US administration's Department of Education has no authority over the operation of schools. Control of the school system rests with the **states** and **local school districts.** There are about 30,000 **local school boards** running the operation of schools, i. e. selecting the teachers, principals and other employees and fixing the salaries.

Most schools are **financed** by a local **property tax.** School boards raise money by taxing local homes or businesses at a certain rate. Since property values differ a lot in different areas, this leads to huge inequalities. Some areas have much more money to fund their schools than others. To compensate for these inequalities **the federal government provides money** for schools and school programmes. In fact, it provides more money than the local districts supply.

The ages for **compulsory education** vary by state. It usually begins at the age of five to eight and ends at the age of 14 to 18. More and more states are now requiring school attendance until the age of 18. In most schools, education is divided into three levels: **elementary school, junior high school** (middle-school) and **senior high school.** On all levels children are divided by age groups into **grades,** ranging from kindergarten and first grade for the youngest children, to twelfth grade, which is the final year of high school.

Post-secondary education in the United States is known as **college** or **university.** It normally consists of four years of study at an institution of higher learning and leads to a bachelor's degree. Graduate studies may follow, especially if the aim is a professional degree such as law, medicine or dentistry.

Students may be educated in **public schools** (state schools), **private schools** or **home school.** In home schooling children are taught by their parents at home.

6.1
Schools

In the US, the term K-12 is used to describe a child's 12 years of schooling from kindergarten to the 12th grade. About 90 % of American children attend free public schools. Schools either follow a 6–3–3 pattern (six grades in elementary school, three grades in junior high school, three grades in senior high school, an 8–4 pattern (eight grades in elementary school, four grades in high school) or a 6–6 pattern (six grades in elementary school, six grades in high school).

6.1.1 State schools

Elementary education

Elementary education starts in **kindergarten,** usually at the age of six. But more than half of all American children aged three to five get some form of earlier education, often at **nursery schools** and **day schools** or **day cares.** A lot of these institutions are private and fee-paying. Elementary schools concentrate on the "three R's" – reading, writing, arithmetic. Subjects taught at elementary schools include English proficiency (reading, writing, spelling and other related skills), science, social science (history and geography) and mathematics.

Secondary education

Secondary education consists of **high school** (junior and senior high school). As in comprehensive schools, all students go to the same school but take different courses according to their talents and abilities. After the 12th grade it ends with **graduation** when students will get their high school diploma. The **core curriculum** usually includes English, science, mathematics, foreign languages and history. This basic curriculum is supplemented with a great number of **"elective" courses.** These courses might include cooking, driver's education and performing arts, to name just a few. **Commercial and vocational courses** like typing and book-keeping or car mechanics and a number of **extra-curricular activities** might also be on offer.

There is **no national exam;** instead, local school districts lay down the standards and exams required.

American high schools tend to offer a very wide range of subjects and extracurricular activities for their students to choose. A day might start with Keyboard Training (learning how to touch type) or Computer Literacy (a course on how to use computers, the Internet and specific software like Word or Internet Explorer). It is followed by "Reserve Officers Training Corps" (ROTC), an elective course that focuses on leadership development, problem solving, strategic planning, and professional ethics. Other classes are Video Production, Drama or Forensics (forensic science, the examination of physical objects).

6.1.2 Private education

Different US administrations have made an effort over the past decades to improve the academic standards at American schools. The decentralized structure of the US education system, however, makes it very difficult to bring about change. States and local school districts might or might not follow the recommendations of the (federal) Department of Education.

Schools in the inner-cities, especially, experience lots of problems. They are under-funded and overcrowded and face problems like violence and drug dealing on a daily basis.

An increasing number of parents, therefore, decide to send their children to **private** or **charter schools** or to **teach them at home.** Roughly 12 % of all children are either tutored at home or sent to private schools. There are schools run by religious groups like the Roman Catholic, Lutheran or Jewish denominations. They are called **parochial schools.** Other private schools are the so-called **"charter schools"** which started in the early 1990s. They use public money, but have more freedom and flexibility than most public schools. The main idea behind charter schools is that they are managed by community members, parents and teachers and allow for new teaching philosophies, their own curriculum and diverse cultural and social lifestyles.

Since compulsory education in the United States means that a child must be educated, but does not mean that this must happen in a school, **home schooling** is legally possible. So parents choose this possibility for different reasons: some will do it for religious reasons, others might not trust the academic achievements of the public school system or might want to avoid the problems of inner-cities schools.

6.2 Higher education

Well over half of all high school graduates go on to some form of higher education at colleges or universities.

Basics **Institutions of higher education in the USA**

- junior or community college (two-year courses)
- technical college (two-year courses)
- liberal arts college (four-year courses)
- university (four-year courses for undergraduates) plus graduate or professional schools for students seeking a Master's (MA) or doctoral (PhD) degree

Most **colleges and universities** offer four-year courses (undergraduate studies) that lead to a bachelor's (Bachelor of Arts (BA) or Bachelor of Science (BS or B. Sc.) degree. **Junior colleges** offer two-year courses that enable students to go on to university or liberal arts college or start a career. **Technical colleges** offer two-year vocational programmes.

Admission to many institutions of higher learning is quite competitive. This is especially true for the "better" and more prestigious universities like the **"Ivy League":** Harvard, Yale, Princeton and others.

Postsecondary education is **not free.** It is quite expensive and puts up a social barrier which is sometimes lowered with the help of public and private grants or scholarships. Despite all of this, it is obvious that students from better-off families can go to better universities.

6.3
US schools in crisis

The American school system faces many **problems.** The most important are:

- The state of **schools in inner-city areas.** Many schools lack money and are understaffed. They have to cope with students that are hostile, disinterested and aggressive.
- A large number of students are **dropouts** who leave school without taking final exams.
- Large volumes of students do not turn up for classes (truancy).
- There are still unsolved racial issues, despite the fact that racial segregation in schools was declared illegal and "bussing" was used for a while to create racially integrated schools. Many schools still reflect white or black neighbourhoods.
- The "old" racial issues (black / white) have further been complicated by the dramatic growth of the **Latino** and the **Asian-American population.**
- Some areas with a large Latino population have introduced **bilingual education,** where the students are taught in both Spanish and English. This was done in the hope that children would overcome their language problem and integration would be easier. Critics doubt this and favour a method of **"English-immersion"** classes.
- Students' academic achievements have declined. Critics of the schools system believe that there are too many elective subjects and that more academic curricula should be taught.

7
Great Britain: Social Structure, Immigration and Social Welfare

Great Britain is still a country where class is more important than in most other countries. Surveys show that class-consciousness is strong and that most people still identify with a particular social class.

As a result of the Industrial Revolution Britain has been divided into three classes: the **upper class,** the **middle class** and the **working class.** It was only after World War II that class differences became somewhat less obvious and **social mobility** – the movement from one class to another – increased. This trend towards a **more egalitarian society** was helped by the common war experience, the introduction of the **comprehensive school,** the foundation of the **Welfare State** and the development of a **mass society** where lifestyles became more similar.

Despite of these developments, class has remained an important factor in social divisions in the United Kingdom today.

7.1
Social class and social stratification

Until the beginning of the 21st century government reports and statistics used a model of **social classification** which included six **social grades** from A to E:

- upper middle class (A): higher management
- middle class (B): intermediate management
- lower middle class (C1): clerical and junior management
- skilled working class (C2): skilled manual workers
- working class (D): semi and unskilled manual workers
- those at the lowest level of subsistence (E): lowest grade workers; people living on social welfare

To reflect social and economic change as well as newer employment patterns, the UK Office of National Statistics produced a more detailed socio-economic classification in 2001, consisting of **eight classes:**

1. higher professional and managerial occupations
2. lower managerial and professional occupations
3. intermediate occupations
4. small employers and own account workers

5. lower supervisory and technical occupations
6. semi-routine occupations
7. routine occupations
8. never worked and long-term unemployed

It is obvious that people are separated into social groups based on their occupation. This marks a trend away from the traditional factors which were used to determine class: **birth, education, lifestyle** and **language** as well as **occupation** and **income.** It also reflects the fact that Britain, like many other modern industrial countries, has undergone important social change.

While the number of workers has drastically declined, the middle classes have grown considerably. There now are more "white collar" workers than before, i. e. people working in offices instead of the factory floor. The service industry has grown significantly and with it the number of people employed in these industries. The highest rise is probably among those working in lower and middle managerial and professional occupations.

7.1.1 Class

The upper class

The upper class consists of a very small but wealthy, powerful and influential group of people. It can be divided into the **"traditional"** upper class (whereby members inherit their wealth and position) and the so-called **"business-elite"** (its members are separated from the middle class by wealth, power, connections and property). The upper class in Britain may be compared to an **exclusive club:** money alone will not buy you membership, family background is more important. Members of the upper class will send their children to well-known public schools and prestigious universities. They hold important positions in society, either in public life or as company or bank directors.

The middle class

As in most modern societies, the middle class – or middle classes – in Britain cover the widest spectrum of people. The middle classes can be divided into four groups:

- **the upper middle class** (higher professionals): typical professions are doctors, lawyers, judges, architects and business executives.
- **the salaried professionals:** typical professions are school teachers, university lecturers, civil servants and local government officials.
- **the white collar workers:** typical jobs are desk jobs and clerical work.
- **the self-employed:** the self-employed will run their own small business (shopkeepers etc.).

The working class

Members of the working class will be skilled or semi-skilled manual workers. **("blue-collar workers")** or will work in administrative jobs **("white-collar workers").**

7.1.2
Class distinction

It is often said that class in Britain is more a matter of **values and lifestyle** than of money or occupation. Important values and behaviours are language (accent, vocabulary), manners, style of dress, taste and educational background.

Basics **Values, lifestyle and class**

Upper/middle class
Members of these classes will probably speak "BBC-English", live in large, detached or semi-detached homes with gardens, read quality newspapers, have an interest in the arts (theatre, cinema), dress conservatively, go on expensive holidays abroad, send their children to "good" schools etc.

Working class
Members of these classes will probably speak a regional accent, live in terraced houses or council flats, read tabloid newspapers, watch TV a lot, go to the pub, go on cheap holidays, send their children to local schools etc.

7.1.3
Language and class

Language or accent has always been one of the main markers of social status in Britain. While a regional accent in Germany will simply tell others where you originate from, but not necessarily anything about your social status, things are different in Britain. **Regional accents** are often associated with lack of education and social background. A strong regional accent of the wrong kind might prevent someone from pursuing a successful career. Some regional accents are considered less acceptable than others. While southern accents are quite acceptable, this is not true for northern accents or London's Cockney dialect.

The most commonly accepted accent these days is "BBC-English", i.e. English spoken by many BBC newsreaders and journalists. It is a fairly neutral, south-eastern accent and is accepted as a sign of a good education.

7.2
Immigration

While up to the 1950s, "class" was the decisive factor in Britain's social structure, this changed with **mass immigration** after World War II. **"Race"** or **"ethnicity"** became increasingly important in the British context and supplemented "class" as dominant factors. The United Kingdom changed from being an Anglo-Saxon into a **multiracial or multicultural society.**

7.2.1 Patterns of immigration

The number of immigrants entering Britain prior to the time after World War II was relatively small. Therefore these immigrants were easily assimilated.

- The 18th and 19th centuries saw some black immigrants.
- The 19th century was dominated by a considerable influx of Irish immigrants.
- The first half of the 20th century saw Jewish and Eastern European refugees entering Britain.
- After World War II/1950s: mass immigration of coloured people from the former colonies, many of them from the West Indies (Jamaica).
- 1960s and 1970s: mass immigration from India, Pakistan and Bangladesh.
- From the late 1980s/early 1990s: people from troubled areas such as former Yugoslavia seek asylum in Britain.
- Beginning of the new century: people from new EU member states (Poland, Lithuania etc.) seek work in Britain.

7.2.2 Britain – a multicultural society

In 2001, the majority of the UK population (almost 60 million) were white (92 %). The remaining 4.6 million (almost 8 %) people belonged to other ethnic groups, for example Chinese, Asian or black British. Indians made up the largest of these groups, followed by Pakistanis, those of mixed ethnic backgrounds, black Caribbeans, black Africans and Bangladeshis.

Basics **Multiculturalism – cultural pluralism**

These terms are often used to describe societies where a wide range of different cultural or ethnic groups live together. In most multicultural societies this is a result of immigration. The terms can also be used to describe government policy: the basic idea is that different groups within society should keep their cultures and identities and interact peacefully with one another.

Between 1991 and 2001 the number of people who came from an ethnic group other than white grew by 53 %. Between 1951 and 2001 the percentage of people born overseas doubled from a little over 4 % to almost 8 %. This development clearly reflects the fact that Britain still has very close ties with her former colonies. The great majority of immigrants come from **Commonwealth countries.**

That Britain indeed is **multicultural** can be experienced in many places. Most non-white ethnic groups are concentrated in certain areas. London is the most popular: 45 % live in London where they make up almost a third of all London residents. Birmingham, Manchester and Liverpool are other cities where one finds large numbers of immigrants. It's in these – and other cities – where the impact of the various cultural and ethnic groups is most obvious: Indian and Pakistani restaurants, black people from the Carribean and Africa, the Notting Hill Carneval, islamic mosques.

But there are also places where the presence of immigrants is hardly felt. Areas like Scotland and Wales have only very small percentages of immigrant population.

The graph shows that around half of the non-white population are Asians of Indian, Pakistani, Bangladeshi or other Asian origins. This reflects Britain's history: the majority of immigrants come from Commonwealth countries and virtually all of them have British citizenship.

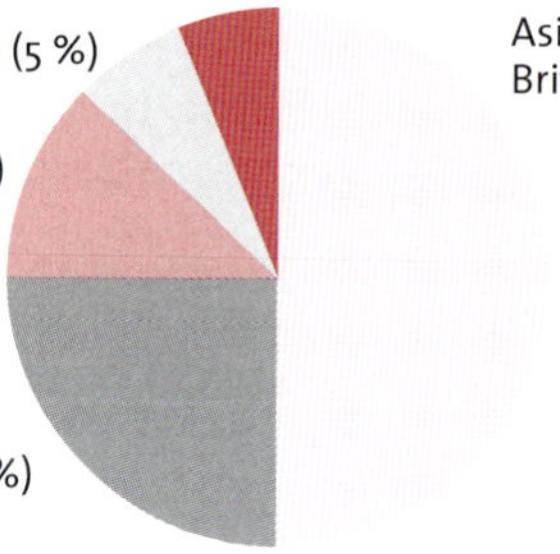

7.2.3
Problems of Britain's multicultural society

If one compares the situation in Germany and Britain as far as immigration is concerned, one will find marked differences.

When mass immigration started in Germany in the late 1950s the reasons were the same as in Britain: there was a big shortage of labour, and people from abroad were needed for the labour market. But it is here that the similarities end. The "Gastarbeiter" who came to Germany were mostly from Southern European countries (Italy, Yugoslavia etc.) and were not all that different in their cultural backgrounds.

Immigrants to Britain, however, came from **completely different cultures and religions.** There were Sikhs, Hindus, Muslims and Rastafarians as well as Christians. They were from **Asia, Africa and the West Indies** and brought with them completely different cultural backgrounds and social values. This made integration very difficult; it also meant that the immigrants rarely united to take a common stand. In fact, there is quite a strong friction between some of the immigrant groups, sometimes leading to street fighting among them.

Although different immigrant groups show different results in coping with the new living conditions (with Indians and Pakistanis doing quite well and black immigrants doing less well), **ethnic minorities in Britain still face a number of common problems** (compared to the non-immigrant population):

- less skilled jobs and lower wages
- higher unemployment rates
- poorer housing conditions
- closed communities, especially in the inner cities
- higher crime rates
- racial discrimination
- harassment (often by the police)

Although these problems still exist, there have been quite a number of improvements, bringing about more equality and integration:

- Second and third generation immigrants are now getting a better education and better jobs.
- African Asians and Indians in particular are more successful as businessmen and shop-keepers.
- There are more immigrants in managerial and professional positions.
- The ethnic minorities are better represented in local government. On the national level there now are a number of Black and Asian MPs.

The government has attempted to decrease racial discrimination and to bring about better relations between immigrants and native British through the **Commission for Racial Equality,** a body that can investigate unlawful practices of discrimination and make suggestions to improve the situation. The **Race Relations Act** of 1976 has made open discrimination in housing and employment illegal.

Despite of all these advances, Britain still has a long way to go on the road of equality. The **race riots** of the past decades (**Brixton** 1981 and **Bradford** 2001, among others), show that there still is a lot of racial tension.

7.3 The Welfare State

In the 19th century there was no system of social security as we know it today. The state did not consider it to be its responsibility to help those in need. Instead, help – if any – came from churches and charitable organisations.

The development of the British Welfare State started in 1911 when politician **David Lloyd George** suggested everyone in work should pay national insurance contribution for unemployment and health benefits.

Basics **Welfare State**

The main idea of the Welfare State is that the state should provide the provision of welfare services to those in need. The state takes on responsibility for the welfare of its citizens, for example by providing a "safety net" of minimum standards of varying forms of welfare (unemployment benefits, health services, old age pensions etc.). Welfare can be provided by the state itself through the taxpayers' money or by a number of independent institutions and services, as is the case in Germany.

The most common model of the Welfare State is a combination of both: some **benefits** are paid directly **by the state** (e.g. family/children allowances), other benefits are paid through a **mutual insurance system** (e.g. unemployment benefits, pensions).

In 1942, the **Beveridge Report** proposed that all people of working age should pay a weekly national insurance contribution. In return, benefits would be paid to people who were sick, unemployed, retired or widowed. This proved to be the foundation of the modern Welfare State in the UK and was later (in 1948) put into practice in the form of the **National Insurance Act,** the **National Assistance Act** and the **National Health Service Act.** A few years earlier legislation was introduced to help families **(Family Allowances Act).**

7.3.1 The British welfare system

The welfare system in the UK consists of

- the National Health Service (NHS),
- social security,
- social services.

The National Health Service (NHS)

Established in 1948, the NHS is a **publicly funded** healthcare system. It provides **free health care** for all UK-residents; foreigners will also be treated free of charge. Care is provided according to people's medical need – not their ability to pay. The large majority of the NHS services and facilities are provided **free of charge,** with over 80 % of the cost paid through general taxation. The remainder is financed through contributions to **National Insurance** by all employers and employees.

Patients normally consult their GP (General Practitioner) who then decides on further treatment by specialists or in a hospital. While this sort of treatment is free, patients have to pay for prescriptions. They also have to make a contribution towards the cost of adult dental treatment, eyeglasses and dentures.

There are private medical insurance schemes in addition to and not instead of, national insurance.

Basics **NHS: problems and changes**

For a long time the NHS was a model for other countries. It was known for its efficiency and egalitarianism. This changed in the 1980s, however, due to an increasing demand for health care and the fact that the NHS was underfinanced at the time. This lead to a number of problems, most noticeably long waiting lists for medical treatment and especially operations, shortages of hospital staff (who were underpaid and had to work long hours). There was a lack of modern medical equipment and hospital buildings were in need of repair and modernisation.

A number of **changes to the NHS** were introduced to improve the situation. These included:

- running the NHS more efficiently, i.e to save money, reduce services and make the remaining services more efficient,
- creating new and modern hospitals,
- employing more NHS staff (doctors, consultants, nurses) and
- making patients pay for some services (dental treatment, eyeglasses).

Social security

The system of social security includes:

- income support
- family allowances
- retirement pensions
- benefits for the sick and disabled
- unemployment benefits

As with the NHS, the costs for social security are paid for by general taxation as well as contributions of employers and employees to the National Insurance.

Social services

Most of these services are aimed at young families with social problems, elderly or disabled people, children and young offenders. The services are provided by professional and voluntary groups and charities such as the Red Cross, the National Society for the Prevention of Cruelty to Children or "Meals on Wheels" and are financed through a system of government aid and donations.

Discussion **Arguments for and against the Welfare State**

The concept of the Welfare State remains controversial. The debate usually centres on the question, how far a state's responsibility for its citizens' welfare should go.

Pros:

- It is a means to fight social injustice and inequality.
- People should not be allowed to suffer unnecessarily through lack of help.
- Not everything should be left to "market forces".
- It is a means to bring about social reform and a more egalitarian society.

Cons:

- The costs of the Welfare State are too high.
- The peoples' responsibility for themselves and their motivation to work is reduced by an "overcaring" Welfare State.
- Social services may be abused.

8
USA: Social Structure, Immigration and Social Welfare

The United States is often called **"a nation of immigrants".** Except for the small group of people that are descendants of Native Americans everybody else has an immigrant background, making the US one of the most **ethnically diverse** countries in the world. Many immigrants left their home countries for a better life in the US and in the hope of realizing the **American dream** – a society where everybody is free to realize one's potential.

There was and is, however, a huge discrepancy between the ideals of the American Dream and America's **social reality.** The United States is neither classless nor egalitarian and not everyone can fulfil their expectations.

Today, American society is made up of many **ethnic groups,** of which many still struggle to find a place in, and its **social structure** is not all that different from other advanced nations, with poverty and economic inequalities.

The American **ideal of self-help and self-reliance** prevented the emergence of a welfare state like in some European countries. It was only in the wake of the **Great Depression** of the 1930s that the US started to introduce some elements of a modern welfare state. There was one important omission, however: the United States still has **no mandatory legal health insurance.**

8.1
Population structure

America is a country of immigrants. Its current population of roughly 305 million people is almost completely made up of immigrants and their descendants.

Basics **Race and ethnicity**

The US population's racial distribution in 2006 was as follows:
- White (excluding white Hispanics): 66 %
- Hispanic or Latino: 15 %
- Black or African American: 13 %
- Asian: 4 %
- American Indian or Alaska Native: under 1 %
- Native Hawaiian or other Pacific Islander: under 1 %

Projections are that by 2050 Non-Hispanic whites will make up 46 % of the total population while the percentage of Hispanics will rise to 30 %. African Americans will make up 15 % and Asian Americans 9 %. These projections throw a light on the dramatic **demographic change** in the US: in 1960 Non-Hispanic whites made up 85 % of the population; by 2060 this group will no longer make up the majority of the population.

US **population growth** is among the highest in developed countries. By 2050 the population is projected to reach 439 million. Most Americans (80 %) live in cities and suburbs. California and Texas are the most populous states, confirming a tendency for the population centre of the United States to move westward and southward.

The United States is a relatively "young" country with more than one quarter of the population under the age of 20 and only 13 % over the age of 65.

8.2 Minority ethnic groups

8.2.1 Native Americans

The terms "Native Americans" and "Alaska Natives" are used to describe the **indigenous peoples** from the regions of North America, now encompassed by the continental United States, including parts of Alaska. They comprise of a large number of tribes, states and ethnic groups, many of which survive as intact political communities.

The colonization of America by European settlers brought about a clash of cultures, due to the great differences between European and native societies. After the establishment of the United States the idea of **civilizing Native Americans and assimilating them into American society** became stronger. Military force **("Indian Wars")** was used to reach these aims. In these wars, many Native Americans were killed, while others died from European diseases. The massacre at **Wounded Knee** in 1890 marked the end of Indian resistance. The tribes were driven from their territories and were forced to live in reservations, which they were not allowed to leave. Parts of the reservations were sold to white settlers by the government. By 1933, the Native Americans had lost about 60 % of their land.

The aim of assimilating Native Americans was only given up in the 1970s. Since then, the government has aided and encouraged self-determination of the tribes. Today, roughly **2.8 million Native Americans** live in the United States, mainly in California, Arizona and Oklahoma, making up less than 1 % of the total population. Many suffer from poor health, poor education, high unemployment and low income. Their land is "held in trust" by the United States for American Indians. It is managed by the **Bureau of Indian Affairs (BIA).** Many Native Americans believe that in respect of the sovereignty of Native American peoples the American government should deal with Native American peoples through the Secretary of State instead of the BIA.

Native American communities have governments that administer services like firefighting, natural resource management and law enforcement.

8.2.2 African Americans

The term **African Americans** (or **black Americans)** is generally used for citizens of the United States who have origins in any of the black populations of Africa. Most African Americans are the direct descendants of captive Africans who survived the **slavery era.** African Americans still make up the single **largest racial minority** in the United States and are the second largest racial group after Whites in the US.

There are nearly **41 million African Americans** in the US. They make up 13.5 % of the total population. In January 2009, Barack Obama became the first African American President of the United States.

History

- **Early 17th century:** The first Africans arrive in Virginia. They work as labourers and have the status of servants who trade several years of labour in exchange for passage to America.
- **18th century:** Towards the end of the 18th century Africans make up 20 % of the population in the American colonies, making them the second largest ethnic group after the English. More and more Africans are sold to America as **slaves** and work on large plantations in the South, where slavery is an integral part of the economic system.
- **19th century:** By 1860 there are 3.5 million enslaved African Americans; another 500,000 live free across the country. In 1833 an anti-slavery movement is founded in the North **("abolitionism").** In 1863, during the **Civil War** between the industrial North and the rural South, President Lincoln signs the **Emancipation Proclamation,** freeing all slaves in states that had seceded from the Union. This is followed by **citizenship** for all black Americans in 1868 and the **right to vote** in 1870. The **Jim Crow laws** in the Southern States enforce **racial segregation** in every area of life, from public transport to schools. The right to vote is suppressed, economic opportunity is denied and acts of racial violence become commonplace **(Ku Klux Klan).** The Supreme Court supports this legislation by its **"separate, but equal"** doctrine. Large numbers of African Americans leave the South for the West or the North.

There has been much progress for African Americans since the days of the Civil Rights Movement. Blacks now are an important factor in US politics. There are now black mayors, black governors and, of course, a black president. However, the blacks are still at a disadvantage economically and socially. Their mean income, for example, is considerably lower than that of whites.

The **biographies** of two leading figures of the Civil Rights Movement – Martin Luther King and Malcolm X – illustrate the common and the different experiences these two men have had as leading African Americans born in the first part of the 20th century. Both were murdered for political reasons.

Biography **Martin Luther King (1929–1968)**

Martin Luther King, Jr. grew up in Atlanta, Georgia as the son of a Baptist Reverend. King got involved in the beginnings of the **Civil Rights Movement** in **1955** when **Rosa Parks** was arrested for refusing to give up her bus seat to a white person. King led the **Montgomery Bus Boycott** which lasted for more than a year and ended with the abolition of racial segregation on all Montgomery public buses.

In 1957, King helped found the **Southern Christian Leadership Conference** (SCLC) which he led until his death. The SCLC organized non-violent protests, strongly influenced by Gandhi's non-violent techniques.

King visited the Gandhi family in India in 1959, deepening his understanding of **non-violent resistance** and his commitment to America's struggle for civil rights. King led and organized marches for the blacks' right to vote, desegregation, labour rights and other basic civil rights. The best known of these marches and campaigns took place in Albany, Georgia (1961/62) and Birmingham, Alabama (1963). The climax came in the summer of **1963** with the **"March on Washington"** where 200 000 protesters heard King give his famous **"I Have a Dream"** speech.

In **1964,** King received the **Nobel Peace Prize** for his work to end racial segregation and racial discrimination through civil disobedience and other non-violent means. Towards the end of his life, King became more radical, arguing that the country needed larger and broader changes, including a better distribution of wealth. This was echoed by his support for the **Poor People's Campaign** in **1968** which tried to address issues of **economic justice.**

On April 3, 1968, King gave his last speech in **Memphis, Tennessee,** in which he said: "And I'm happy, tonight. I'm not worried about anything. I'm not fearing any man. Mine eyes have seen the glory of the coming of the Lord." On the next day, **April 4, 1968** King was shot while he was standing on the balcony of his motel.

In 1986, **Martin Luther King, Jr. Day** was established as a US national holiday. It was first officially observed in all fifty US states on January 17, 2000.

The Civil Rights Movement

The Civil Rights Movement between 1954 and 1968 was directed at abolishing racial discrimination against African Americans, particularly in the southern United States. It was – at least in part – sparked off by a Supreme Court decision in 1954 which declared that the segregated schools were contrary to the Constitution.

A number of groups fought to end discrimination and inequality and to achieve full civil rights for African Americans:

- the National Association for the Advancement of Colored People (NAACP): legal defence for black Americans
- the Congress of Racial Equality (CORE): freedom rides, sit-ins
- the Southern Christian Leadership Conference (SCLC): non-violent action, – "passive resistance" (protest marches, sit-ins, boycotts); Martin Luther King
- the "Black Muslims" (Nation of Islam): for African culture and against integration; Malcolm X
- the Black Panther Party: militant, "violence against violence", against integration

Biography Malcolm X (1925–1965)

Malcolm X was born as Malcolm Little in Omaha, Nebraska. By the time he was 13, his father had died and his mother had been committed to a mental hospital. After living in a series of foster homes, X became involved in the criminal underworld in Boston and New York. In 1945, he was sentenced to eight to ten years in prison.

While in prison he took an interest in reading and became a member of the **Nation of Islam,** a group which preached black self-reliance and opposed black integration into white society. When he was paroled in 1952, he met **Elijah Muhamed,** the leader of the Nation of Islam and changed his surname to "X", thus replacing his white slavemaster name of "Little". He became one of the Nation's leaders and the public face of the Nation of Islam.

While the civil rights movement fought against racial segregation, Malcolm X advocated the complete **separation of African Americans** from white people. He proposed the establishment of a separate country for black people as an interim measure until African Americans could return to Africa. Malcolm X also rejected the civil rights movement's strategy of non-violence and instead advocated that black people use any necessary means of **self-defense** to protect themselves.

In 1964 he left the Nation of Islam over a conflict about its religious teachings. He travelled to Mecca and visited Africa as well as Europe. In the United States he was one of the most sought-after speakers on college campuses. He was threatened by the Nation of Islam; his house was burned down.

On **February 21, 1965** Malcolm X gave a speech to a meeting of the Organization of African Unity in Harlem where he was shot by a man with a sawn-off shotgun.

Chronology Civil Rights Movement – important events

1955 Bus boycotts in Montgomery, Alabama, against segregation in buses.
1961 Freedom rides to end segregation in public transport.
1962 First black student enrols in the University of Mississippi.
1963 March on Washington. M. L. King's "I have a dream" speech.
1964 Civil Rights Act bans discrimination in public accommodation and work.
1965 Voting Rights Act makes voting registration easier. Malcolm X murdered.
1968 Martin Luther King assassinated.
1970 "Bussing" starts to encourage desegregation in schools (ends 1976): white children are brought to schools in black areas and vice versa.
1972 Equal Opportunity and Employment Act: "positive" discrimination to promote better opportunities for ethnic minorities.

8.2.3 Hispanics

Most Hispanics (or Latinos) come from **Mexico, Puerto Rico** or **Cuba.** About **45 million Hispanics** live in the United States, making up roughly 15 % of the total population. They are the largest and fastest growing ethnic immigration group.

Mexican Americans are the largest group among Hispanics in the US. They are often called **Chicano.** Immigration from Mexico started in the middle of the 19th century; the numbers, however, were relatively small. It was only in the second part of the 20th century that the number of legal and illegal immigrants from Mexico increased considerably. Most Chicanos live in the border states. Most Mexicans come to the US in the hope to improve their situation. As a group, Chicanos are economically deprived, have a low level of education, low incomes and a low social status.

Puerto Ricans enjoy a special status. As nationals of the US commonwealth Puerto Ricans have US citizenship, although Puerto Rico is not as state of the US. Most of them live in New York and New Jersey in relatively poor economic conditions.

Cubans are an economically successful group of immigrants. The started to leave Cuba for the Unites States for political reasons when Fidel Castro took power in 1959. Most of them live in Florida and many of them enjoy middle-class status. Their political influence – especially with regard to US foreign policy for Cuba – must not be underestimated.

As an ethnic group, Hispanics do not assimilate well and many stick to their own language. This is the first time in US immigration history that the largest single group of immigrants speaks just one language – Spanish. Another problem lies in the fact that Hispanics tend to live in ethnic enclaves and do not want or are not able to assimilate. There are now parts of the United States where Spanish has become the predominant language. This is echoed in the growing number of Spanish speaking radio and TV stations and bi-lingual schools.

8.2.4 Asians

Asian Americans include sub-ethnic groups such as **Chinese** Americans, **Filipino** Americans, **Indian** Americans, **Vietnamese** Americans, **Korean** Americans, **Japanese** Americans and others whose national origin is from the Asian continent. There are a little over **15 million Asian Americans,** making up 5 % of the US population.

Asian Americans make up the second largest racial minority in the United States. They have the lowest poverty rate and the highest educational attainment levels, median household and median personal income of any racial group.

Asian Americans are the most recent group to immigrate to the United States in large numbers. Their immediate **economic success** in the US makes them stand out from other immigrant groups and shows a clear difference to early 20th century immigrants. Asian Americans tend to live in metropolitan areas, mainly L. A., San Francisco, New York, and Chicago. About half of them live in Hawaii or California.

Some refer to Asian Americans as a **model minority** because of their economic success and high educational qualifications, while others see this as stereotyping.

8

8.3 Social class and social stratification

There is considerable controversy regarding social class in the United States. Some even claim that "social class" does not exist in the US or that the large majority of Americans are in the same class, the middle class. Many believe in a simplified three-class model that includes the "rich", the "middle class" and the "poor". It is true that social classes in the United States have less distinct boundaries than in many other developed countries.

If one applies the usual "markers" for class (income, wealth, education, social status), social stratification in the US can be described in the following terms:

Class	%	Characteristics
capitalist class	1 %	top-level executives, leading politicians, heirs; Ivy League education common
upper middle class	15 %	highly educated; salaried professionals, managers
lower middle class	30 %	semi-professionals and craftsmen, white collar; some college education
working class	30 %	clerical and blue collar workers; high school education
working poor	13 %	service and low-rung clerical workers, some blue collar workers, high risk of poverty; some high school education
underclass	12 %	limited or no participation in the labour force, rely on government transfers; some high school education

Basics **Income**

Income is one of the attributes most commonly used to determine a person's class status. Instead of personal income, household income is often used as a social "marker". In 2005 the overall mean (average) household income was roughly $ 46,000, based on persons aged 25 or older. The **distribution of income among different ethnic and social groups:**

Asian: $ 57,000 Hispanic: $ 34,000
White: $ 49,000 Black $ 30,000

These figures show that there is a large difference in household income among the different ethnic groups, with Asians being particularly successful and Blacks being the least successful group. If one **relates household income with educational qualification** the results are as follows (2005):

- some high school: $ 23,000
- high school graduate: $ 37,000
- some college: $ 46,000
- bachelor's degree or higher: $ 73,000
- master's degree: $ 78,000
- doctorate degree: $ 97,000
- professional degree: $ 100,000

The degree of social inequality in the United States can – up to a point – also be measured by the **poverty rate,** i.e. the number of people that are considered to be poor by the country's standards. While the overall poverty rate in the US is not considerably higher or lower compared to other developed countries, the difference between the poverty rates of various ethnic groups shows that there are still groups whose risk of poverty is much higher than others.

Basics **Poverty in the United States**

Poverty is usually measured by the **poverty line** set by the US government. It is expressed in absolute terms. In 2008 a single person was considered to be below the poverty line if he or she did not have more than roughly $ 10,000 a year.

About 36.5 million people were considered to be poor in the United States in 2006, a little over 12 % of the total population. These poverty rates were among some of the ethnic minorities (in 2001): Blacks (22.7 %), Hispanics (21.4 %), Asian and Pacific Islanders (10.2 %).

As far as America's regions are concerned, the South had the highest poverty rate (13.5 %). Among people living inside central cities the poverty rate was 16.5 % while it was 14.5 % amongst people living outside metropolitan areas. Worst hit were families with a female householder and no husband present, with a poverty rate of 26.4 %.

8.4 Immigration

America was – and still is – shaped by the process of continuous immigration. There is probably no other country in the world where almost any inhabitant could claim to be an immigrant or to have descended from immigrants from all over the world. Those immigrants left their homelands because they fled religious persecution, famine and hardship or dictatorships and came to America for a better life. Ireland, England, Germany, Italy, Scandinavia, Poland, Russia, Asia, Mexico and Cuba are just some of the countries that immigrants came from.

Immigration today

Current immigration rates are moderate. About ten million people settled in America as legal immigrants in the decade between 1991 and 2000. Since 2000, legal immigrants to the United States number approximately one million per year, of whom about 600,000 are change of status immigrants who are already in the US. Illegal immigration may be as high as 1.5 million per year with a net of at least 700 000 illegal immigrants arriving each year to join the 12 to 20 million that are already there. Most illegal immigrants are Hispanics, many of them entering the US by crossing the Mexican-American border.

Basics **Historical periods of immigration**

- **Early immigration (17th / 18th century):**
  The first European settlers arrived in the early 16th century. They settled along the north-eastern coast. The **Pilgrim Fathers** on their ship **The Mayflower,** landed in **New England** in **1620.** This marks the beginning of the building of the American nation. This first wave of immigrants were mainly English, Scots and Germans.
- **Mass immigration in the 19th century:**
  The 19th century was the century of European immigration. The **early part of the century** saw mainly immigrants from **Britain, Ireland** and **Germany** come to America. The potato famine in Ireland in the 1840s caused hundreds of thousands of Irish to leave their country. The second wave of immigrants came in the **second part of the century:** new groups of immigrants came from Scandinavia and China. At round the **turn of the century,** the third wave included newcomers from southern and eastern Europe, among them many immigrants from Italy, Greece, Poland and Russia.
- **Immigration in the 20th century:**
  Although the end of World War I halted the uncontrolled influx of immigrants, immigration itself did not come to an end. The **middle years of the 20th century** saw a multitude of nationalities entering the US. Many of them were refugees escaping fascism in Germany; others left an impoverished post-war Germany. In the **second half of the 20th century** most immigrants were Asians and Hispanics.

Legal immigration is today **regulated** by law through the 1990 **Immigration Act** (IMMACT). It limits the annual number of immigrants to 700,000 and emphasizes that family reunification is the main immigration criteria, in addition to employment-related immigration.

These days, **illegal immigration** is a **major political issue** in the United States. There are **two main political positions:** the first wants to provide for legalization and amnesty of those present in the country illegally. The second wants to crack down on employers that hire undocumented workers and build a wall along the Mexican border to stop the illegal entry of immigrants via one of only two land borders.

8.4.1 American dream, melting pot and salad bowl

The **American dream** has often been quoted as a major factor in attracting immigrants to the United States. According to historians, the rapid economic and industrial expansion of the US was not simply a function of being a resource-rich, hardworking and inventive country, but also the belief that anybody could get a share of the country's wealth if he or she was willing to work hard. Another contributing factor was the absence of a rigid class structure.

Basics **The American dream**

"Work hard and you will achieve prosperity" – this is the essence of the American dream. It is influenced by the Protestant work ethic (see page 70), which believes that it pleases god if people work hard and make money. The idea of the American dream puts responsibility squarely on each individual's shoulders: it's up to you if you are successful in life; it's your own fault if you don't make it.

The American dream is both **myth and reality.** For many the old cliché "from dishwasher to millionaire" still holds a promise and for a few it still holds some truth. American success stories like the one about the young weight lifter who came to the US in the late 1960s, with little else but his will to succeed and became a movie star and then a national political figure, still happen. However, there is also a darker side to the American dream: for every individual or group that "makes" the American dream there are thousands of others that don't.

Criticism of the American dream

The concept of the American dream has been criticized a lot; the main criticism being that it is misleading. These critics believe that there are many reasons why it is impossible for each and every individual to be "successful" in life through determination and hard work. This criticism has been very much a part of American popular culture. Arthur Miller's play *The Death of a Salesman* and the film *Easy Rider* are two well-known examples.

Melting pot and **salad bowl** are two metaphors or analogies to describe the social structure of the United States in relation to the success or failure to assimilate the millions of immigrants into American society. While it is widely believed that the early groups of immigrants assimilated fairly well and became "American", this is not believed to be true for those who came to America in the second part of the 20th century. These groups did not assimilate easily and kept much of their own cultural identity.

Basics **Melting pot**

The term **"melting pot"** is a metaphor: people from different cultural backgrounds are thrown into a pot (America) and processed in it; as a result all assume a new identity as Americans. It stands for the idea that newcomers to a country assimilate, i. e. give up most of their original cultural identity and assume the cultural identity of their new home country. The term is sometimes used to describe the concept that in the United States "individuals of all nations are melted into a new race of men".

Basics **Salad bowl (or mosaic)**

The term **"salad bowl"** is also a metaphor: people from different cultural backgrounds are thrown into a salad bowl; although they become part of a new entity/product they do not mix but keep most of their original flavours/identities. This means that newcomers to a country do not assimilate but keep their original cultural identity. The term is sometimes used to describe the reality of multiculturalism in the United States.

Historically one can argue that the "older" groups of immigrants that came to the United States in the 19th and early 20th century were mainly of the melting pot type. Between 1820 and 1960, a total of 42 million people immigrated; 34 million were from Europe. **Immigrants from Europe** – Irish, Italian, German, Scandinavian and others – were assimilated into American society without completely losing their cultural roots. There still are strong communities of Irish-Americans or Italian-Americans today. But the "Irish" or "Italian" title only shows where they originally come from; there is no doubt that these groups would primarily define themselves as American.

With the "newer" groups of immigrants that immigrated in the second part of the 20th century, things were different. Coming mainly from **Asia and Latin America,** these immigrants assimilated far less easily into American society. The majority of them kept strong cultural ties with their countries of origin, especially the language. In some parts of the American South, Spanish is now a second language that is spoken in many schools and on radio and TV stations. These immigrants are part of America's **multicultural** salad bowl.

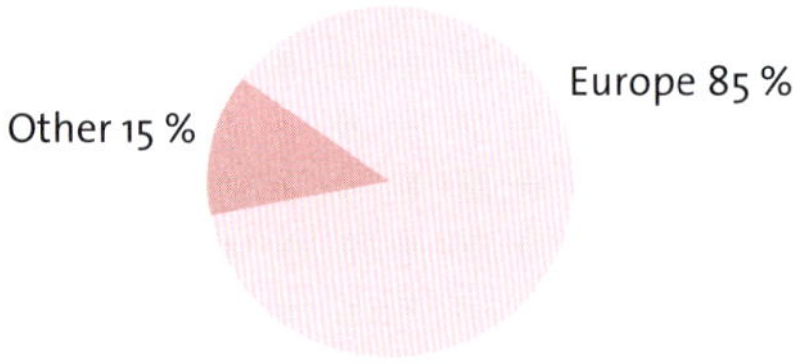

Percentage of foreigners by region of birth 1900

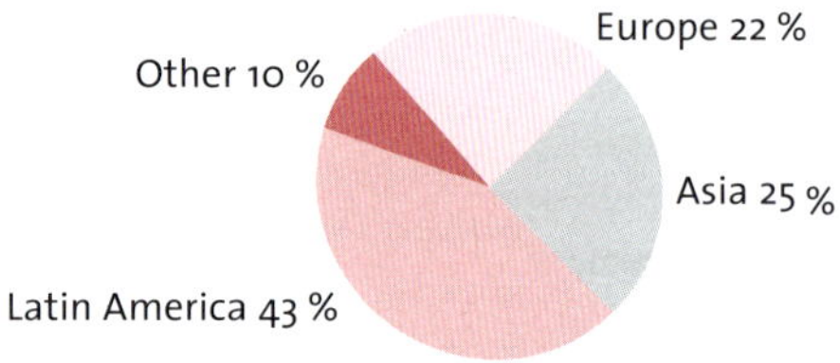

Percentage of foreigners by region of birth 1990

In 2004, approximately 34 million people in the USA were foreigners. Of these, almost five million were born in Europe, close to nine million in Asia and well over 18 million in Latin America, with two and a half million born in other areas of the world. This clearly shows the recent trends of immigration to the US: the majority of immigrants – many of them so-called illegal aliens – come from Latin America, in particular **Mexico.**

8.5 Social welfare

It can hardly be said that the US has developed a genuine welfare system. Although **social security** was introduced in the context of the Great Depression and President Roosevelt's **New Deal** in 1935, when many millions of Americans were hit by unemployment and poverty, the US **does not provide basic medical insurance for all its citizens** up to the present day. This is due to the American concept that the state should not cover everybody's life "from cradle to grave" but that everyone is responsible for him- or herself.

Basics **Social security**

The **Social Security Act of 1935** established a social insurance to help and protect the elderly and pay unemployment benefits. This insurance is funded through payroll taxes paid by those in employment and their employers.

Today, **social security** is the largest federal programme and the single greatest expenditure in the federal budget. Social security covers:

- **pension:** everybody is paid a small pension, regardless of their financial situation.
- **unemployment benefits:** they are normally paid for six months and amount to about half of the previous income.
- **Medicare:** health insurance for the aged and disabled persons.
- **Supplemental Security Income (SSI):** a welfare programme which ensures that even people who had never paid into the system can get a pension.

A side effect of the social security programme in the United States has been the near-universal adaptation of the programme's identification number, the **social security number,** as the national identification number in the United States. Although no one is required by law to have a social security number, nearly everybody has one, since it is used by government agencies as well as many other institutions (banks, colleges etc.) as a **personal identifier.**

Basics **Health care**

Although health care is very expensive, it is not mandatory to have health insurance in the US. There are, however, programmes such as **Medicare** or **Medicaid** which provide basic health insurance to elderly, disabled and poorer residents. For most Americans, health insurance is provided as an employee benefit, while unemployed, part-time, and self-employed workers must pay for their own insurance. In 2004 **45 million people in the United States (15.6 % of the US population) had no health insurance coverage.** Even those who are covered by one of the health care programmes often have to pay some of the costs out of their own pockets or have extra private insurance.

This has always been considered by many to be one of the most important social problems in the US. Medical bills, for example, are a leading cause of bankruptcy in the United States, with many people going broke because they cannot pay their medical bills.

There have been numerous efforts to provide universal health care in the 1960s and 1990s. They all failed in the face of strong opposition from politicians who objected to government control of medicine and business groups which opposed further regulation of the healthcare and insurance industries. It is still not universally accepted that availability of broader health care should be considered a right and be paid for by public funds in the United States.

Welfare programmes

Welfare programmes are outside the social security and are financed by the federal government. Today over $ 300 billion are spent each year on welfare programmes. The most important ones are:

- **Medicaid:** a health-care programme for the poor,
- **Childcare,**
- **food stamps:** vouchers to buy food more cheaply,
- **free school meals,**
- **public housing:** subsidized rents for apartments and
- **the Temporary Assistance for Needy Families (TANF):** welfare recipients must take part in community service, vocational training or work experience in order to qualify for time-limited welfare-payments.

The debate over welfare

Welfare is one of the big "partisan" issues in the United States, meaning that the division runs along party lines.

- **The Republicans** tend to believe that expensive welfare programmes are at least part responsible for unemployment and high government spending. They hold the opinion that lower taxes and less government spending will improve the economic situation by motivating people to buy more goods and increase production. This will lead to more jobs and help the poor and unemployed more than welfare programmes do.
- **The Democrats** believe that the state should help those in need as best as it can. Government funded welfare programmes are therefore a necessity. One of the main aims of the Democratic Party is to bring about a better health care system, making sure that all Americans are protected for life against the hazards of ill health. This must also apply to the uninsured.

A shift in the tradition of welfare programmes took place in the 1990s when the Democrats introduced a system called **"welfare to workfare".** This limited the time for which welfare benefits can be received and put an emphasis on re-integrating people into the world of work.

9
Great Britain: Religion

Since Britain is a predominantly Protestant country, one might think there is a great degree of religious unity. This is only partly true. There is a surprising variety of denominations in Britain, both Christian and Non-Christian. **Christianity** is the most prevalent religion with over 70 % of the population and the **Church of England** has by far the largest Church membership with over 18 million.

Among **Non-Christian religions** the most numerous are Muslims, Sikhs, Hindus and Jews. Religion in Britain has suffered a decline in the past decades due to a continued secularisation of British society.

9.1
Christian religions

The Church of England

The Church of England (Anglican Church) is the officially established church in England. It considers itself to be both **Catholic** and **Reformed.** It regards itself as in continuity with the pre-Reformation state Catholic church, but has been a distinct **Anglican** church for centuries and is partly influenced by the Protestant Reformation.

The **British Monarch** is the formal Head of the Church and holds the title "Defender of the Faith". The Queen appoints archbishops, bishops and deans on the advice of the Prime Minister. The spiritual leader of the Anglican Church is the **Archbishop of Canterbury,** Primate of all England. He is considered to be the head of the worldwide communion of Anglican Churches. In practice the Church of England is governed by the **General Synod.** Senior bishops of the Church of England sit in the House of Lords.

There are two branches of the Church of England:

- **High Church** (Anglo-Catholics): similar to Catholics in church ritual and the authority of the clergy
- **Low Church** (Evangelicals): simple church services and a greater importance of the Bible and preaching

The Church of Scotland ("Kirk")

It is recognized in law as the national church of Scotland, but is independent of state control in spiritual matters. The Church of Scotland is strongly influenced by the Scottish Reformation (Calvinism) and is a Reformed church.

The Church in Wales

The Church in Wales is a member of the Anglican Communion. It is not an established church.

Basics **Anglican Church between Catholicism and Protestantism**

The Anglican Church has a middle position between Catholicism and Protestantism:

- The **liturgy,** the formal ritual of worship, resembles that of the Catholic Church, although it is not in Latin, but in English.
- Up to a relatively short time ago there was no ordination of women; this changed in 1992, when the General Synod allowed for the **ordination of women as priests.** In 2008 the General Synod approved the ordination of women as bishops.
- The Anglican Church **does not recognize the supremacy of the Pope.**
- Marriage is not a sacrament like in the Catholic Church.

9.2 Non-Christian religions

Mainly due to immigration, there are now large communities in Britain representing non-Christian religions.

Muslims are by far the largest group. The estimated **2.4 million Muslims** make up the second largest religious group in the United Kingdom. There are hundreds of mosques and community centres for Muslims all over the UK. The **Muslim Council of Britain** is an umbrella organisation for many local, regional and specialist Islamic organisations in the United Kingdom.

Other large denominations include **Judaism** – Britain has the second largest Jewish population in Europe –, **Sikhism** and **Buddhism.**

10
USA: Religion

The United States has an unusual position compared to other post-industrial countries. While there is normally a relatively high percentage of people claiming to have no religious beliefs, this is not true for the US. The number of people claiming to have no religious beliefs is rather low there. Many say that religion plays a **very important role** in their lives.

More than 75 % of adult US citizens identify themselves as Christians. There is a **great variety of Christian denominations,** with the Roman Catholic Church as the largest single denomination and the Southern Baptist Convention the second largest. There are over 2000 different denominations and some 500,000 churches, temples and mosques all over the USA.

Some of the original Thirteen Colonies were established by English settlers who wished to practice their own religion without discrimination. They were the Quakers, the Roman Catholics and the Puritans. Some of the colonies had official public religions until the end of the 18th century, when the **separation of church and state** was introduced and all official religions were disestablished.

Main religious preferences of Americans (2002):

- Christian: 78.5 %
  - Protestant: 65.4 %
  - Roman Catholic: 30.4 %
  - Mormon: 2.2 %
  - other Christian: 2.0 %
- Jewish: 1.7 %
- Buddhist: 0.7 %
- Muslim: 0.7 %
- unaffiliated/none/other: 18.4 %

10.1
The Puritan heritage

Many of the early settlers were Protestants with a **Puritan** or **Calvinist** background. Puritanism/Calvinism is associated with a number of religious groups. The **Puritans** believed that the English Reformation of the 16th and 17th centuries had not gone far enough. The **Calvinists** were influenced by the teachings of the French reformer John Calvin and others in the 16th century.

Basics **Important Puritan/Calvinist beliefs**

Some important Puritan/Calvinist beliefs that influenced the United States a great deal were:

- The **Protestant work ethic:** material success is achieved through the virtues of hard work, thrift and self-discipline. It pleases God if individuals are materially successful through the exercise of these virtues, which encourage the individual to save and to invest money instead of spending it on personal pleasures. Many believe that these are the values a developing capitalist society needs and that these values played an important part in the development of industrial growth and business in the United States, especially since the Protestant work ethic had an influence on many religious groups in America.
- The notion that **America** is the **"promised land",** especially blessed by God, goes back to the Puritans who saw themselves as a "chosen people".
- The notion that wealth is not an aim in itself but should also be given away to help others explains the long tradition of **charity** in the USA.

Characteristics of religious communities in the USA

Some of the characteristics of religious communities in the USA are:

- Churches in America do not rely on state subsidies or the taxpayers' money, but rely on donations from their members or money generated through fund-raising activities.
- Religion is not officially taught in American schools. If a school offers religious education, it has to take place outside the school building.
- There are no religious public holidays in the US. This reflects the strict separation of church and state.

The Electronic Church

Televangelism is a phenomenon of contemporary religious life in America. The term "Televangelism" was coined by Time Magazine in the late 1990s and consists of the two words television and evangelism. It describes the use of television to communicate the Christian faith.

When TV was deregulated in the second part of the 20th century and everybody with enough money could access the television networks, religious TV and radio programmes were seen as a means to reach many people. These programmes are often used not only to present religious messages, but also to entertain. Now there are even TV networks such as **Trinity Broadcasting** or **The God Channel.**

Some pastors do not have a conventional congregation as such and solely work through television.

10.2
A new fundamentalism?

Christian fundamentalism has been growing in importance in the US since the 1970s. Often also called the **Christian Right,** it marks a surge of Christian fundamentalists towards politics.

It is a form of "religious revival" and is characterised by a number of things:

- The movement is very **conservative** and fights against the modern "permissive society". It is against abortion, pre-marital sex, pornography, homosexuality, "obscene" rock songs and feminism.
- Fundamentalists are **creationists:** they believe that God literally created life and they oppose the teaching of Darwinist evolution theory in American schools.

11
Great Britain: Mass Media

With the emergence of the „Information Age“ in the final decade of the 20th century the mass media have undergone dramatic changes. This is mainly due to **technological advances in broadcasting and the development of the Internet.**

The introduction of digital satellite TV, digital cable TV, digital terrestrial television and IPTV ("Internet Television") has led to a multitude of channels, both free and pay TV. In Britain there are up to **600 channels** for consumers plus a number of services offering **on-demand** content.

The Internet is about to replace traditional media like the "box" (TV) or the newspaper as the most important source of information or entertainment, at least for many younger people. The communication industry is the most dynamic industry in the world; no other industry creates more jobs.

11.1
The press

The British newspaper market consists mainly of the **national press,** i.e. national daily newspapers ("dailies") and national Sunday newspapers ("Sundays") that are sold nationwide. Although there are regional and local papers, they have relatively little significance compared to regional markets like Germany where most newspapers cater for a certain region only. While there are only five newspapers in Germany that are read nation-wide, e.g. *Bild, Frankfurter Allgemeine, Die Welt,* there are ten national dailies and nine Sundays in Britain. Reading a voluminous Sunday paper on Sunday morning is part of the British culture.

Nearly all the dailies and Sundays are produced in London. Most of the papers had their offices in **Fleet Street,** the "Street of Ink" in central London. In the 1970s, the first newspapers left Fleet Street and moved to new office sites in the **Docklands** area as industrial printing plants could be developed there more economically. The printing presses use very modern technology. It became much easier and less costly to use colour. This is one of the reasons why all papers use colour for both text and photographs today. Another reason is the fierce competition among the papers.

11.1.1 National newspapers

Basics **The national dailies: traditionally divided into three groups**

- **quality papers,** often called "broadsheets" because of their large size
- **popular papers,** often called "tabloids" because of their smaller size or "red-tops" because of their generous use of red in their titles
- **mid-market papers,** i. e. papers that fall in between the two previous categories

Quality papers

The quality papers like *The Times, The Guardian, The Independent, The Financial Times* and *The Daily Telegraph* are read by the more educated classes and publish reliable news and background information, both on national and international affairs. Some of the qualities have introduced more compact formats, closer in size to the tabloids than the broadsheets.

Popular papers

The popular papers cost less than the quality papers and concentrate on sensationalist news and "human interest" stories. Most of their readers belong to the lower middle classes and the working class. They use bigger print, especially in their headlines, and more colour than the qualitiy papers. The *Sun* is famous for its topless "Page Three Girl". Among the best-selling tabloids are *The Sun, The Daily Mirror and The Daily Star.*

Mid-market papers

Mid-market papers are *The Daily Mail* and *The Daily Express*. They are tabloids that cover the intermediate market.

Sunday papers

The same division into groups is true for the Sunday papers. The Sunday **quality papers** are *The Sunday Times, The Sunday Telegraph, The Independent on Sunday* and *The Observer.* The Sunday **populars** are the *News of the World, The Sunday Mirror* and *The People,* while *The Mail on Sunday* and *The Sunday Express* cover the **mid-market.** One typical feature of the Sundays is their sheer volume and weight. All the Sundays include not just one, but numerous **colour supplements,** dealing with topics like sports, the arts, travel, food, wine or leisure activities. Because all this content would be too thick and cumbersome in tabloid form, the Sunday papers have tended to keep their broadsheet format.

The difference between quality papers and red-tops reflects the still existing – and some believe widening – gap between Britain's social classes.

11.1.2
Monopolies, political leanings and the right of privacy

There are strong **monopolistic tendencies** in the British newspaper market. Five "Press Lords" or newspaper groups control about 90 % of the total circulation of the national press. The best known of the "Press Lords" is Rupert Murdoch, originally from Australia, whose firm News International owns *The Times, The Sunday Times, The Sun* and the *News of the World*. Murdoch owns about one third of the British national press. He also owns TV Stations and other papers world-wide.

A majority of the national papers supports the Conservative party. This is considered to be a problem since it puts Labour at a disadvantage in general elections.

Because of the fierce competition between newspapers in the UK, some newspapers concentrate on sensationalist journalism which often invades the privacy of people. This has led to an increasing number of complaints to the Press Complaints Commission which was brought into existence to watch over press standards in Britain.

11.2
Radio and television

Similar to the situation in Germany, where public broadcasters like ARD and ZDF and private corporations like RTL and Sat1 or ProSieben share the market for radio and television, there are two main authorities in Britain that are responsible for television: the BBC (British Broadcasting Corporation) and Ofcom (Office of Communications).

11.2.1
The British Broadcasting Corporation (BBC)

The **BBC** was founded in 1922 and is the world's oldest and biggest broadcaster. The BBC is funded by a television licence fee that all households with a television must pay. It offers two **analogue** TV channels – BBC One and BBC Two – as well as a number of **digital** services, e. g. BBC Three, BBC Four, BBC News and BBC Parliament. The BBC also runs five national radio stations called Radio 1 through Radio 5 as well as many local and specialised radio stations, both analogue and digital.

BBC One offers general interest programmes such as news, current affairs, sports, documentaries and light entertainment while **BBC Two** specialises in intelligent yet popular programme genres like documentaries, art films, plays and educational programmes.

The radio stations are all aimed at particular groups of listeners, with **Radio 1** serving a younger audience and **Radio 3** catering for those with an interest in classical music and the arts. As the BBC is financed by the **licence fee** there are no commercials interrupting the programmes.

Basics **Most watched programmes in 2007 (BBC One)**

1. *East Enders* (a daily soap)
2. *Doctor Who* (a long-running science fiction series)
3. *The Vicar of Dibley* (a sitcom)
4. *Concert for Diana* (held at Wembley Stadium in memory of Princess Diana)
5. *Strictly Come Dancing* (a show featuring celebrities with professional dance partners competing against each other)

The list shows that the original division between public and commercial television – the BBC standing for more serious and educational programmes and the commercial channels standing for light entertainment – is no longer true. Under the pressure of the commercial channels, the BBC had to appeal to a wider audience. It is no coincidence that the most-viewed programmes in both systems are **daily soaps:** *East Enders* (BBC) and *Coronation Street* (ITV).

11.2.2 Commercial television and radio

Commercial television in the United Kingdom started in 1955. Since 2003 **Ofcom** (Office of Communications) is responsible for licensing and regulating Britain's commercial television services. The oldest and most popular is **ITV** (Independent Televison). Before the emergence of digital TV in the 1990s there was just **ITV** and **Channel 4** to compete with the BBC.

Today there are a large number of commercial TV stations in Britain. With the development of cable and satellite technology, which made it possible to broadcast many digital programmes, private companies entered the British TV market.

The biggest and best-known satellite programmer is **BSkyB** (British Sky Broadcasting). BSkyB, owned by Rupert Murdoch who also owns *The Times* and the *Sun* newspapers, operates **Sky Digital,** a subscription television service in the UK and Ireland. BSkyB has nearly ten million customers in the UK and Ireland and is Britain's largest pay TV provider, comparable to (the much smaller) Premiere in Germany.

11.2.3 Recent changes

Analogue terrestrial television was the traditional way of receiving television in the UK. However, it has now largely been supplanted by digital providers. Analogue televison will come to an end in the UK in 2012 when the last of the analogue transmission will be switched off. It is being replaced by a number of technologies:

- digital terrestrial television (available in the UK since 1998),
- cable television (a subscription service normally bundled with a phone line and broadband internet access),
- satellite television (either freesat or pay TV),
- IP television (IPTV) (using the Internet infrastructure to broadcast TV) and
- mobile television (using 3G mobile phones to receive TV signals).

12
USA: Mass Media

Circulation figures of well-known daily **newspapers** in the US like *USA Today, The New York Times* or *The Wall Street Journal* are considerably lower than those of the best-selling popular dailies in the UK. This has to do with the sheer size and the federal character of the US, but also with the fact that Americans tend to get their information about current events from watching television. Although there are papers that are read across the nation, there is **no true nationwide press.** Instead there are a huge number of regional papers, printing regional and local news that have no place in the TV news programmes. There are well over 2,000 daily and Sunday papers, a lot of them part of big **newspaper chains.**

Radio and television in the US is similarly fractured. There are over 12,000 radio stations, most of them commercial. Television is dominated by **big networks** like *CBS* or *NBC* which provide programmes for hundreds of regional and local TV stations. Practically all of American TV is **commercial** and financed through advertising, except for the Public Broadcasting Service (PBS) with approximately 300 stations which is financed by the Federal Government and sponsors.

12.1
The press

Over the years **newspapers** have become less important in the US. Their circulation has declined and they are reaching less people than before. Although there is no real "national" newspaper, the following daily newspapers are of national importance and are sold in most US cities:

- *USA Today* (popular, broad audience)
- *The Wall Street Journal* (financial and general news)
- *The New York Times* (probably America's most influential newspaper)
- *The Los Angeles Times*
- *The Washington Post*

Most of the other daily newspapers are of regional or local importance only.

Apart from daily and Sunday papers there a number of quite influential weekly **newsmagazines,** namely *Time, Newsweek* and *U. S. News and World Report*.

The **freedom of the press** is guaranteed in the First Amendment of the Constitution. Over the past decades, parts of the press have taken over the role of watchdogs concerning morals and decent behaviour, digging deep into the lives and personal conduct of politicians, film stars and others. The best known example in recent years probably is "Zippergate", President Clinton's affair with a young female White House trainee. This affair got so much publicity that it even lead to the (unsuccessful) **impeachment** of the President.

Investigative journalism is another hallmark of the American press. It shows how important a free press is in controlling the government. The most famous examples of this kind of investigative journalism was the Watergate affair.

Basics **Watergate (1972)**

Two *Washington Post* reporters (Carl Bernstein and Bob Woodward) found out that burglars who broke into the Democratic Party's election headquarters in the Watergate Hotel in Washington had connections with the CIA and the White House. They proved that people very close to President Nixon were involved in the planning and execution of the burglary and that Nixon himself was aware of illegal attempts to cover up the affair. The pressure on **President Nixon** got so strong that he **resigned** before he could be impeached. It was the first resignation of a president in US history.

12.2 Radio and television

In the United States there are three basic types of television:

- **broadcast** or "**over the air television**", which is freely available,
- **cable television** and
- **satellite television.**

The latter two require a paid-for subscription to receive. Most American households receive cable TV.

12.2.1 Television networks

The United States has a decentralized and predominantly commercial television system. There are no national broadcast programming services. Instead, there are hundreds of local TV stations, which often are affiliated to or owned by one of the major TV networks: **NBC, CBS** and **ABC.**

Some TV stations are **independent,** i.e. they are not affiliated with the big three networks. They produce some local content but rely mainly on **syndicated** shows, often reruns of old TV series and movies, which they buy directly from the production companies without going through one of the major networks.

Apart from the "big three" networks there are some others. The **Fox Broadcasting Company** started in 1986 and now challenges the big three networks with popular shows like *The Simpsons* and sports.

Due to the large number of **Hispanics** living in the US there now are a number of Spanish language stations like **Univision,** which is the fifth-largest network, **Telemundo** and **TeleFutura.**

Basics **Programming**

Programming is very similar among the networks and its affiliates. A typical weekday **schedule** might look like this:

Morning:
- early-morning news show (local content)
- early-morning network news show (e.g. NBC's *Today,* mixing news, weather, interviews and music)
- syndicated programming (talk shows etc.)

Afternoon:
- syndicated soap operas
- syndicated talk shows such as *The Oprah Winfrey Show*

Evening:
- local news
- national network news programme
- syndicated programmes

Prime Time (prime time content is provided by the networks):
- comedy programmes
- reality TV shows
- dramas like *CSI, Grey's Anatomy, Desperate Housewives* and so on
- late night shows like *Late Show with David Letterman*

In addition to the big "broadcast" networks a number of **cable and satellite networks** exist. Top **cable networks** include USA Network, Versus (Sports), MTV, Fox News, Disney Channel and Discovery Channel, but also HBO (Home Box Office) and CNN. Satellite networks are Dish Network and News Corporation's DirectTV.

12.2.2 Non-commercial television

There is no state-owned or state-influenced broadcasting authority in the US. The federal government does, however, subsidize **public television.** Since the state subsidies are not enough, public television stations also rely on corporate sponsorships and viewer contributions.

American public TV stations concentrate on educational, cultural and public affairs programming. Most stations are affiliates of the **Public Broadcasting Service** (PBS) and share programmes like *Sesame Street*.

12.2.3 Radio

While traditionally most commercial radio stations in the US were affiliated to the major networks like NBC or CBS, they are now controlled by media conglomerates like Clear Channel Communications and many others.

The number of radio stations runs into the tens of thousands, broadcasting both in the **FM** and **AM** bands. Most **FM stations** are music stations, each of them specialising in certain music formats like "Country and western", "Oldies", "Religious" or "Top 40". **AM stations** often broadcast talk and news shows. **Talk radio,** a relatively new format, in which celebrities and experts from various fields answer listeners' "call-in" questions and offer their advice on various topics, has become extremely popular in recent years.

13
USA and GB: International Relations

If we look at the United States' and the United Kingdom's **international standing** today, we can see that America is the world's only remaining superpower, while Britain is one of the bigger European countries, set apart from most other European countries by the fact that it is an island and that it is a (minor) nuclear power.

This was very different at the beginning of the 20th century. Before World War I the United States was a big country of minor international importance, while Britain was a relatively small country of major international importance. It was the most powerful country in the world, with an empire that covered one-fifth of the globe.

Things changed, however, in the course of the 20th century. **America** gave up its isolationist politics, took part in two – mainly European – wars and had become a leading world power by the end of World War II and was determined to keep its influence on world politics. **Britain,** on the other hand, had been reduced to becoming a European power, having lost most of its colonies in the year before and after WW II.

However, Britain's influence on the world can still be felt. English has become the lingua franca of the world, the British political system has been "exported" to many countries, the Commonwealth still plays an important role and the influence of British culture and values is strong.

13.1
America and the world

The United States' role in international politics has often been governed by one of two attitudes: isolationism and involvement. For most of the 19th century the US kept out of international politics, which at the time meant mainly European politics.

Monroe Doctrine

In 1823, President James Monroe first stated the Monroe Doctrine, one of the most important documents of American foreign policy. In it, he declared that the United States of America would not interfere in European wars or international dealings, and in turn, expected Europe to stay out of the affairs of the New World. He claimed that the western hemisphere was never to be colonized again and any attempt by a European power to oppress or control any country in the western hemisphere would be considered a direct threat to the US. America's message to the world was clear: the Americas (both North and South America) are our sphere of influence. Keep out and **"leave America to the Americans".**

From local to global power

The end of the 19th and the beginning of the 20th century marked the United States' shift from a purely local to a more global power. The US started to **increase its economic influence** (economic imperialism) and its overseas expansion. Cuba, Puerto Rico, the Philippines and Guam were annexed and an addition to the Monroe Doctrine, the 1904 Roosevelt Corollary, proclaimed a right for the United States to intervene to stabilize weak states in the Americas. The US had asserted its regional hegemony.

World War I

It was only during World War I that the United States gave up its traditional position of isolation and neutrality. It entered the war in 1917 after Germany had declared unlimited warfare and sunk US merchant and passenger ships. After the war President Wilson succeeded in establishing the League of Nations. He was defeated by the United States Senate, however, which rejected membership in the League of Nations and favoured the "traditional" isolationist policy. As a result the US reverted back to neutrality after the end of World War I for another couple of years. It was only in the context of World War II that the US got permanently involved in international politics.

World War II

Although reluctant at first the US finally decided to join the war in Europe against Nazi-Germany in 1941, motivated by Japan's attack on **Pearl Harbour** and Germany's declaration of war on the United States. The fact that the US entered World War II was the decisive factor in bringing down fascism.

The results of World War II changed the political map of the world: Germany was defeated, other European nations like Britain and France lost their status as world powers and the Soviet Union got a hold on Eastern Europe and became the world's second superpower. Unlike after World War I the US decided to stay in Europe for good.

The Post-war period: Cold War and Détente

The new world order that emerged after World War II was a bipolar one. It was dominated by **two superpowers** – the Soviet Union and the US –, of which both tried to expand their spheres of influence and possessed huge amounts of nuclear arms.

Basics **Vietnam**

To fight the Soviet Union's growing influence in South East Asia the US got involved in Vietnam in the early 1960s. What was meant to be a very reduced military involvement at first turned into an outright war lasting almost a decade. It was the war the US couldn't win. Nearly 60 000 American soldiers were killed. In 1973 the US withdrew its troops. Vietnam turned out to be the American trauma of the 20th century. The Vietnam war also led to disillusionment about America's role as the "world police".

The competing interests of the two vastly different systems soon led to confrontation and "Cold War", to the arms race and almost to "hot war", as in the Cuban Missile Crisis of 1962. In military terms the time was characterized by the confrontation between the main military pacts – NATO and the Warsaw Pact. This period of confrontation between the Soviet Union and the United States basically lasted until the great turning point of the late 1980s and the early 1990s. At times this confrontation was rather harsh as in the Berlin Crisis of 1961 or the Cuban Missile Crisis of 1962. At other times the friction lessened, like in the late 1960s and during the 1970s when there were a number of successful treaties controlling the arms race and bringing about Détente, a general reduction in the tensions between the Soviet Union and the United States.

After the collapse of the Soviet Union

When the East-West-Conflict came to its surprising end with the downfall of the Soviet Union in 1991, the US suddenly found itself in the position of the only world superpower. It played an active role in the international conflicts that followed the end of the Soviet Union and the end of the bipolar world. At that time it looked as if the United States was prepared to act in accord with their European and other partners.

America is likely to play this role for the foreseeable future. This is not necessarily America's choice. As long as a stable new world order does not emerge, the US is left in the position of the world's strongest power. Whether it will continue to act on its own or in cooperation with its partners remains to be seen.

Basics **Nine-Eleven**

The terrorist attacks on the World Trade Centre on September 11th, 2001 deeply shocked America and changed US foreign policy. More than before the US acted on its own. This became obvious when President Bush decided to attack Afghanistan in 2001 and Iraq in 2003 as part of his **"war on terrorism".**

War on terrorism

The term "Bush Doctrine" is sometimes used to describe various related foreign policy principles of the years after 2001. Initially, the phrase described the right of the United States to secure itself from countries that give shelter to terrorists or help them. This is why **Afghanistan** was attacked in 2001.

Later the Bush Doctrine also included the controversial policy of **preventive war,** which said that the United States should overturn foreign regimes ("rogue nations") that represented a potential threat to the security of the US. Iraq was attacked in 2003 on the ground that it threatened US security through its programme of producing weapons of mass destruction. All in all, the foreign policy of the Unites States in the first decade of the 20th century became more and more **unilateral,** meaning that the US was willing to act on its own, without even consulting its allies in the world.

The war in Iraq has shown that it is much easier to win a war than to win the peace. The Iraq war has also started a widespread controversy in the US. It seems that a majority of Americans wants the troops to retreat. **President Barack Obama** has promised to bring the troops back successively.

13.2 Empire and Commonwealth

In the late 19th century Queen Victoria could claim, "the sun never sets" on her **empire.** At its height in the 1920s the British Empire covered about a quarter of the landmass of the earth and 400–500 million people lived under British rule. It was the largest empire in history and, for over a century, was the greatest global power.

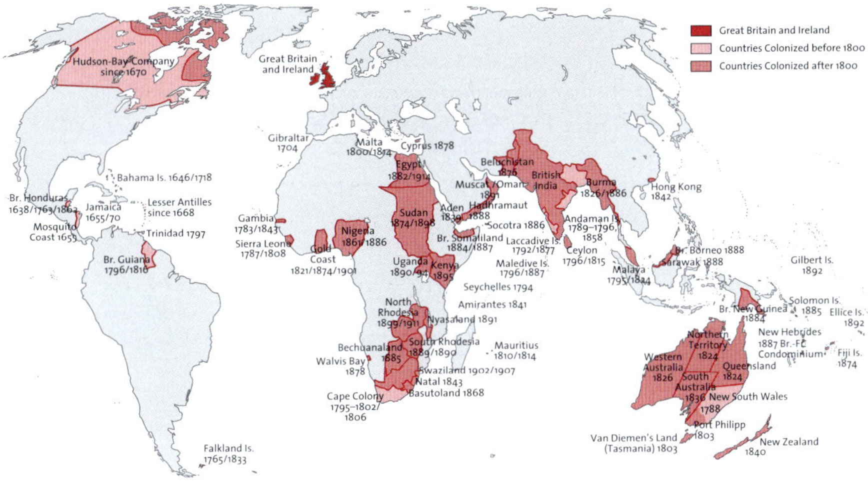

The growth of the British Empire

13.2.1 From Empire to Commonwealth

After World War II Britain's Empire dissolved as one colony after the other became independent. However, this did not mean the end of Britain's relationship with her former colonies. Today Britain and most of her former colonies are members of the **Commonwealth,** a voluntary association of independent states.

The First British Empire: 16th to 18th century

The beginnings of the Empire date back to the 16th century when British seafarers like Sir Francis Drake put to sea to seek immediate profits. In the 17th century, Britain concentrated on the Americas, setting up colonies in North America and the Caribbean. Initially, the Caribbean provided England's most important and lucrative colonies, later to be replaced by the Thirteen Colonies in North America.

The 18th century saw the settlement of Australia, which started out as a penal colony in 1788.

The East India Company was established in 1600 to trade with Asia. Near the end of the 18th century, when Britain lost its colonies in Northern America after the American War of Independence, the First British Empire came to an end.

The Second British Empire: 19th century to World War I

While many of the early colonies were mainly seen as a source of cheap raw materials and markets for British goods and thus were only of economic interest to the mother country, this perception started to change in the 19th century. It was replaced by **imperialist** thinking.

Basics **Imperialism**

Imperialism is often defined as the **practice of extending the power, control or rule by one country over areas outside its borders.** The controlled areas are formally declared to be its colonies or protectorates. Sometimes the form of control is less formal: the dominant country can also influence or control the subordinate area or country economically or politically, without using military force.

The Second British Empire is one of the best known examples of imperialist policy in history. Britain enlarged its empire by means of conquests, diplomacy, commerce and purchase. Its main aims were to extend British rule over large territories and gain political, military and strategic advantages. This does not mean that there were no economic interests involved; they were just augmented by other interests.

In the 18th century British expansion shifted from the Americas to Asia and Africa. Britain took possession of India – Queen Victoria was proclaimed Empress of India in 1876 –, Ceylon, Burma, Malaysia and Hong Kong.

The late 19th century saw Britain and other European nations in the "scramble for Africa". Competing with countries like France and Germany, Britain became the most successful colonial power in Africa: it held control over South Africa, Egypt, Nigeria and other African colonies, comprising almost 30 % of Africa's total population.

13.2.2 Decolonisation

The end of World War II signalled the end of the Empire. Britain had to concentrate on its domestic problems after World War II while at the same time anti-colonial nationalist movements challenged British rule in most of its colonies. First India, then other territories in Asia and Africa demanded – and finally got – independence from Britain. This process marked the Empire's transformation into todays' Commonwealth.

13.2.3 The Commonwealth today

The Commonwealth is a loose confederation of independent nations, most of them former members of the British Empire. There are 53 countries in the Commonwealth with a total population of around 1.5 billion people. Queen Elizabeth II. is (symbolic) Head of the Commonwealth; she is also head of state in 16 countries.

Australia, New Zealand and South Africa followed in the early years of the 20th century. In India, 1947 was the year of independence: the British finally withdrew as a result of the passive resistance put up by the supporters of Mahatma Gandhi. Other nations followed, and the end of the British Empire saw the emergence not only of the Commonwealth but also of a **postcolonial world** with problems of its own. The fight for national liberation in the second half of the 20th century has changed the political maps of Asia and Africa.

Basics **Political aims of the Commonwealth**

The political aims of the Commonwealth were put down in the **Harare Declaration** of 1991. Member states are expected to

- promote democracy, the rule of law, good government and human rights,
- promote the equality of women,
- provide universal access to education,
- promote economic development and ease poverty,
- take action against disease and illegal drugs and
- support world peace and the United Nations.

The **Commonwealth Secretariat** in London coordinates the international cooperation of the member states and prepares regular meetings of the head of states of the Commonwealth countries.

Language is also an important factor. Because of their colonial background and their shared histories with Great Britain, English is still the first or official language in most states of the Commonwealth.

13.3 The colonial and post-colonial experience

The topic of the colonial and post-colonial experience is closely related with Britain's past and present. It starts with the process of colonization in the 18th and 19th centuries and continues up to the present. It looks at the experiences of the colonizers and the colonized, at a time when Britain was the world's greatest imperialist power and ruled large parts of Africa as well as India and many other places. It also looks at the way the different cultures interacted at that time and how they interact today in a multicultural Britain with millions of immigrants from the former colonies.

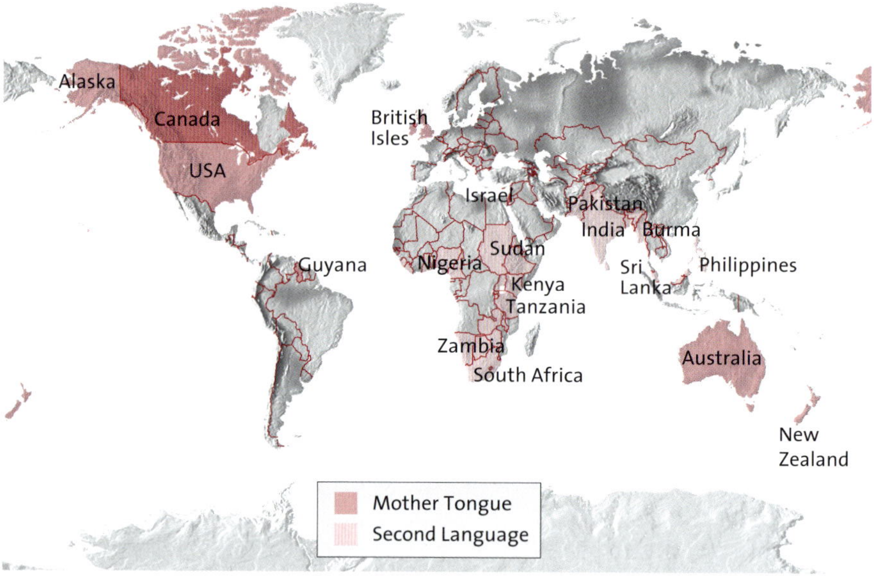

English-speaking countries of the world

Basics **Imperialist ideology**

When Britain set out to build its empire, the country was faced with the problem of justifying the conquest of other countries and ruling these countries by force. Among the most common justifications were:

- **Biological argument:** there are different races in the world, some races are superior (white Europeans), others are inferior (Africans, Asians and others).
- **Religious arguments:** Christianity is the only true religion, Christians have the duty to convert the rest of the world.
- **Cultural arguments:** Europeans are superior to the "natives", they bring civilization to the less developed parts of the world, this is good for the "natives".

13

After the fall of the British Empire these justifications were more and more criticised and were generally considered to be myths. The social Darwinist perception of a set of superior and inferior races was discredited and people realized that the concept of different races was not scientific but social and political. The Christian involvement with colonialism and slavery and its disrespect for indigenous cultures had opened a huge credibility gap. The idea that the **white man** had taken up a **burden** to serve the colonized people and improve their standing was now seen as a means to hide the true motives for imperialist expansion: to find new markets for products and capital. This process of pointing out the true motives for colonialism and imperialism is sometimes called "post-colonial deconstruction" of imperialist ideology.

Basics **Post-colonialism**

Post-colonialism is about dealing with the **legacy of colonialism.** Post-colonial theory deals with many issues of societies that once were colonies, among them
- the dilemma of developing a national identity after the experience of colonial rule,
- the ways in which writers from colonized countries attempt to articulate and even celebrate their cultural identities and reclaim them from the colonizers,
- the ways in which the literature of the colonial powers is used to justify colonialism through the conservation of images of the colonized as inferior.

Post-colonialism is also about the impact colonialism has on the former colonizing countries like Britain and the impact **immigrants** from former colonies have on Britain today.

As a literary theory post colonialism deals with literature produced in countries that were once, or now are, colonies of other countries. It also deals with literature written by authors who have their origins in former colonies but now live in one of the colonizing countries, e.g. Britain. In general terms post-colonial theory studies the interaction between European nations and the societies they colonized.

Issues and topics in post-colonial studies
- the effects of colonization on both the colonizers and the colonized
- the influence of colonial education, science and technology on post-colonial societies and their development and modernization
- the development of post-colonial identity after the departure of the colonizers
- the question whether decolonization has been possible as a reconstruction free from colonial influence

Central to the theory of post-colonialism are a number of concepts that reflect the main problems concerning the interaction between colonizers and colonized.
- **Diaspora:** when people leave their home country and live as a minority in another country they live in diaspora. They often feel alienated in their new country of residence and do not know what their identity is.
- **Hybridity:** people from former colonies now living in Britain sometimes both try to keep their original identity and to adopt to the culture of the country they now live in. They are influenced by two cultures.
- **Acculturation:** this describes the process of one culture (usually the "native" culture) gradually being replaced by another culture (usually the "dominant" culture of the colonizers). An "old" identity slowly disappears and a new identity emerges.
- **Ambivalence:** this describes the simultaneous rejection and attraction in people of the "other" culture ("otherness"). A person experiencing this kind of ambivalence might be attracted to a person from the "other" culture while at the same time rejecting the culture this person comes from.

Britain is a country where the post-colonial experience is particularly strong. As a multicultural society consisting of a white European majority and a sizeable minority of immigrants from mainly former colonies, modern Britain is a place where the interaction between the cultures of the (former) colonizers and the (former) colonized happens every day. However, this interaction brings with it a number of problems, e. g. racial conflicts, racial and ethnic prejudice, conflicts between different generations of immigrants and the politics of restricting immigration.

13.4 Britain and Europe

Britain has always played a somewhat special role in Europe. First it was kept from joining the European Economic Community twice because France vetoed Britain's application both in 1963 and 1967. When Britain finally joined the EEC in 1973, it was only after a lengthy public debate in Britain about the merits of joining the EEC. Britain has been a member of the EU for over 30 years now but is one of the few member countries that did not join the Euro zone. Public opinion about the merits of EU membership is still divided, probably more so than in other EU countries.

Chronology	Britain and Europe: important dates
1963	Britain applies for membership of the EEC. President de Gaulle of France vetoes the application on claims that Britain's ties with both the Commonwealth and the USA were too close.
1973	Britain is finally able to join the EEC.
1974	The British people confirm this in a referendum.
1991	Britain is among the few members of the EU that do not join the EMU (European Monetary Union). The main reason for not joining the single European currency is the fear of a loss of national sovereignty.
2005	Tony Blair is held responsible by many for the collapse of the EU summit in June regarding the EU's budget over the coming years.
2009	In the wake of the economic crisis, the UK is facing the threat of entering a deep recession following the collapse of the housing market and rising oil prices. Nevertheless, Gordon Brown affirms that Britain is still not ready to join the European single currency.

Europe – a megastate?

There is widespread fear in the UK that the EU is heading in the direction of becoming a mega- or super state, thereby reducing the importance of the individual nation state and its sovereignty. While there is relatively little opposition against the economic implications of the European Union – i.e. the single European market –, opposition against the idea of a politically united Europe with powerful European institutions is fairly strong.

Basics **Euromyths**

Many people believe in so-called *euromyths*. These are pieces of information about the EU that are untrue and often describe the EU as a rather bureaucratic institution trying to regulate everything. The popular press quite often twists the facts in order to strengthen some peoples' fears about the EU.

One such euromyth is that all ambulances throughout the EU must be painted yellow or that builders will not be allowed to take their T-shirts off during work.

The euro debate

Nearly two thirds of British voters are "eurosceptics" or "europhobes". Particularly strong is the opposition against the euro. The two major parties are divided on the subject. While the Labour Party supports the idea of joining the single currency, it also makes it quite clear that Britain will only introduce the euro if this step is considered to be in Britain's economic interest. The Conservatives are against the single currency because they consider the economic risks of joining the euro zone too great. Business in the UK is mainly for the euro. A lot of firms export their goods to euro zone countries. With different currencies these firms run a currency risk which they hope to avoid by becoming a member of the euro zone.

13.5 Anglo-Irish relations

For most of the past centuries, Anglo-Irish relations have been very difficult. Although there have been very close ties between the neighbouring islands, the relationship was not based on equality. For over 800 years, Britain dominated Ireland, making it its first colony. All attempts by the Irish to free their country from British rule were squashed and Ireland never had much of a chance to escape its poverty.

This only changed at the beginning of the 20th century, when Britain finally realized it had to give up Ireland, at least the bigger part of it. Ireland had become a sovereign state, but the island was still divided, with Ulster remaining a part of the UK.

From the late 1960s to the end of the century Ireland experienced "The Troubles", a social and political conflict over the rights of the Catholic minority in Ulster. The 1990s – the so-called Celtic Tiger years – saw Ireland's rapid development from one of the poorer countries in Europe to one of the wealthiest. At about the same time, a political solution was found for the conflict in Ulster.

13.5.1 History

Up to the beginning of the 20th century, **Ireland** was **Britain's oldest colony.** British domination of Ireland had its beginnings in the 12th century when Anglo-Normans invaded Ireland and occupied an area near Dublin called "The Pale". For centuries this remained Britain's only stronghold in Ireland.

Protestantism

The conflict that can still be felt today started in the **16th century** when Britain's monarchs of that time attempted to **establish Protestantism** in Ireland against the fierce opposition of the people of Ireland who were determined to remain Catholics.

In order to gain a better control over the island, Queen Elizabeth I and King James I sent English and Scottish settlers to Ireland at the beginning of the 17th century, mainly to the northern province of Ulster. The native Irish were driven from their land which was given to English and Scottish settlers on a large scale. This colonisation, the **"Plantation of Ulster",** can be considered the beginning of the **Ulster conflict.** A period of bitter hostility between the Irish and the British had begun. In this conflict "Irish" can be defined as "native", "catholic" and "oppressed", while "British" can be defined as "colonizer", "oppressor" and "protestant".

As the colonization of Ireland by the British went on, the Irish were put more and more at a disadvantage. Laws were introduced that excluded Irish Catholics from school and public offices. Many Irish lost their land to British landlords and had to make a living as tenants. In the **"Act of Union" 1801,** Ireland became part of the "United Kingdom of Great Britain and Ireland". The discrimination against the Irish was eased a bit under the **"Catholic Emancipation Act"** of **1829.**

Great Famine

The 19th century was a time of extreme hardship for the Irish. In the 1840s the failure of the potato crop for several successive years led to the **Great Famine.** Millions of Irish either died from starvation (potatoes often were the sole nourishment) or left the country, starting a period of mass emigration, mainly to the US and Britain. During that time Ireland lost half its population. It is only now, at the beginning of the 21st century, that roughly as many people live in Ireland as there lived before the Great Famine.

Nationalism and rebellion

Also during the 19th century, Irish Nationalism became stronger. The **Fenian Movement** stood for land reform, political autonomy and, ultimately, Irish independence. There were a number of unsuccessful rebellions against British rule. In 1914 a **Home Rule Bill** giving the Irish political autonomy found a majority in the House of Commons but was immediately suspended because of the outbreak of World War I.

A coalition of Irish nationalists consisting of the newly founded Irish Republican Army (IRA), the Irish trade unions and many intellectuals attempted to revolt against British rule in the **"Easter Rising"** of **1916.** The rebellion was brutally crushed by the British and the leaders of the rebellion were executed. This led, in turn, to a guerrilla war between the Fenians and the British military.

Partition and Civil War

The British government realized that the situation in Ireland had become uncontrollable. The **"Ireland Act"** of **1920** therefore allowed for the division of the country into a politically autonomous southern part and the north (Ulster) which remained part of the United Kingdom. Radical Irish nationalists did not accept this solution and a **civil war** broke out between moderate and more radical Irish nationalists. The moderate nationalists, prepared to live with the partition of the country, won that war.

Free State

The **Anglo-Irish Treaty** of **1921** granted part of Ireland Independence. The island was split up into four provinces: the predominantly catholic provinces of Leinster, Munster and Connacht became the **Irish Free State,** the predominantly protestant province of **Ulster** remained part of the "United Kingdom of Great Britain and Northern Ireland". The Irish Free State left the Commonwealth in 1949 and became the **"Republic of Ireland".** The Republic is often referred to as the "26 counties" while Ulster is often called the "six counties".

Situation today

The Republic of Ireland has about four million inhabitants. Most of them (95 %) are Catholics. The country has been a member of the European Union since 1973. Traditionally one of Europe's poorest countries, Ireland has now become one of Europe's wealthiest nations.

Northern Ireland has about 1.5 million inhabitants. The majority of the population is Protestant ($^2/_3$), but there is a substantial Catholic minority ($^1/_3$). The conflict in Northern Ireland over the past decades (see "The Troubles") was about Protestant domination and the rights of the Catholic minority.

13.5.2 "The Troubles" in Northern Ireland

For centuries Ireland has been one of Europe's poorest countries. Until fairly recently this was still true. To many people Ireland was a romantic place of great scenic beauty – the "Emerald Isle" or "Green Isle" –, with world-famous writers like James Joyce. Also, Ireland has a long history of being conquered by foreigners and a somewhat shorter history of mostly unsuccessful rebellions against its conquerors. To others, Ireland was a place where a civil war with strong religious overtones took place since the late 1960s – "The Troubles" were all over the news.

Basics **"The Troubles"**

The conflict in Northern Ireland – often referred to simply as "The Troubles" – is an old one. For 30 years, from its beginnings in 1968 to the **Belfast Agreement** in **1998,** it has dominated the lives of the people of Northern Ireland as well as British and Irish politics and has cost thousands of lives.
There are many misconceptions about this conflict, mainly about it being a religious conflict. Although religion certainly plays an important part in the conflict, it is **not a conflict about religion.** The roots of the conflict go back far in Ireland's troubled history and have a lot to do with the fact that Ireland was Britain's first colony. The conflict is also about migration, settlement and "ethnic cleansing". And last, but not least, it's a **social conflict** about discrimination, inequality and civil rights.

The peace process

The Belfast Agreement of April 1998 – often referred to as the Good Friday Agreement – marks the beginning of a difficult and lasting effort to end violence in Northern Ireland and find a permanent political solution for the province.

Basics **The Good Friday Agreement**

A key element of the Good Friday Agreement is the devolution of some central government power in Northern Ireland to a Northern Ireland Assembly, a regional parliament, and the formation of a Northern Ireland Executive, a regional government. The concept of power sharing is central to both the Assembly and the Executive, i. e. representatives from both communities must be part of both institutions.

The first Executive started work in early 1999 but in October 2002, the British government suspended the Northern Ireland Assembly and brought back direct rule because of unresolved conflicts over **weapons decommissioning** – i. e. the surrender of arms by both loyalist and republican paramilitary groups –, which was one of the major stumbling blocks in the peace process. These conflicts have now been brought to an end.

Since the Good Friday Agreement all parties involved in the conflict – i. e. The British and Irish governments as well as nationalist and loyalist organisations – have tried hard to stop all violence and find a workable compromise that is acceptable to the "two communities" in Northern Ireland.

Basics **Power sharing**

In 2005 the IRA declared an end to its armed struggle and started giving up its arms. This opened the way for a new **power-sharing executive** for Northern Ireland. In early March 2007 elections for the Northern Ireland Assembly at Stormont were held and resulted in a victory for the two major parties: the Democratic Unionist Party/DUP; protestant) and Sinn Fein (nationalist; catholic).

At the same time the British government set a deadline: by the end of March an agreement had to be found among the two parties to set up a power-sharing executive (government) in Northern Ireland. The two parties just managed to meet that deadline. The new executive under the leadership of Ian Paisley (DUP) and Martin McGuiness (Sinn Féin) came into effect in May 2007.

The peace process in Northern Ireland took nine long years. Despite of this the situation in Northern Ireland shows that it is possible to stop sectarian violence even after 30 years of bloodshed. It also shows that political solutions are possible.

13.5.3 The Celtic Tiger

Ireland's image in the world started to change with breathtaking speed in the early 1990s. Ireland experienced its **economic miracle** and the country was transformed. Today Ireland is **one of the wealthiest countries in Europe;** per capita income in the Republic of Ireland is now higher than in Germany. In Northern Ireland "The Troubles" slowly came to an end, further improving Ireland's image in the world.

Basics **Celtic Tiger**

The term "Celtic Tiger" (which is used for both the period of time and the country during that period) was coined in the 1990s to describe the rapid economic growth of the Republic of Ireland between the early 1990s and 2002. It is an analogy to the term "tiger states" or "little tigers" which was used to describe countries in South East Asia like South Korea or Singapore during their period of rapid growth in the 1980s.

Among the **consequences** of the "Celtic Tiger" years are:

- **Economic progress:** incomes are up considerably while unemployment is at a very low level. The national infrastructure is constantly improved. This is especially true for roads and public transport.
- **Social change:** while Ireland has traditionally been a country of emigrants this trend has been reversed. There are now more people immigrating to the country than leaving it. Ireland is becoming more urbanized; more and more people are leaving the rural areas for the bigger cities. The importance of religion in Ireland has been reduced. Ireland is becoming a more secular country. Divorce is now possible, homosexuality was legalized, the country had two women presidents in succession and lifestyles have become very similar to the rest of Europe.
- **Cultural change:** the Irish music scene is no longer dominated by traditional groups like *The Dubliners* but by internationally highly successful groups like *The Cranberries* or *U2*. *U2*'s lead singer Bono even was an (unofficial) candidate for the post of president of the World Bank and has regular meetings with important world leaders.

Among the **causes** for Irelands **economic miracle** are:

- the country's membership of the European Union since 1973 which gave Ireland access to European markets, in addition to EU subsidies
- low wages, a well-educated, English-speaking labour force, low taxes and a system of government grants which made it attractive for high profile companies like Intel, Dell or Microsoft to locate in Ireland
- the Belfast Agreement that brought growing stability to Northern Ireland and signalled a likely end to "The Troubles"

Economic aspects of modern Ireland

Ireland's economy has long been dominated by agriculture. This is a thing of the past. **Industry** is the most important sector now, contributing 46 % to the Gross Domestic Product (GDP), almost 80 % to exports and employing close to 30 % of the labour force. Industry in Ireland is largely made up of well-known **international firms,** a lot of them operating in the **high-tech** sector. Ireland is the world's largest exporter of software and is also home to many producers of computers and computer equipment. A quarter of Europe's computers are made in Ireland by firms like Dell and IBM. One of Intel's largest and most advanced **fabs** is located just outside Dublin.

The tertiary sector provides most of the input for economic growth. Apart from **tourism,** which has a long tradition in Ireland, it is call-centres, service operations and finance that dominate this sector. Both Apple and IBM located their European customer service operations in Ireland due to the availability of a young, well educated, English speaking workforce and a good communications infrastructure. Many people calling a service hotline in Europe or the US are in fact put through to a call centre in Ireland.

In 2008/2009 Ireland was particularly hard hit by the worldwide **financial and economic crisis.** For the first time in almost two decades of continuous economic growth and generous state and private spending, the county's economy experienced serious difficulties: economic growth came to a halt, state (and private) debts went up considerably and unemployment increased.

13.6 Globalization

The effects of globalization are all around us. Communication has never been easier: the Internet makes it possible to access information on a world-wide basis and communicate in real-time with people all over the world. In a way, geographical distance has become meaningless. Mobile communication is spreading almost everywhere.

Consumers all over the industrialized world find a similar supply of goods. International brands and multinational corporations like McDonalds, Microsoft, Nestlé or Nike are found on every highstreet. What we eat and what we wear are products of globalization.

Cultural differences do not vanish completely, but a new globalized cultural identity is emerging. This is most evident among the younger generation. Music, films and TV play an important part here. Lifestyles converge; young people in Germany live similar lives to young people living thousands of miles away.

In many ways the idea of the world as a "global village" or a "world society" has become reality and the aspects of globalization are various:

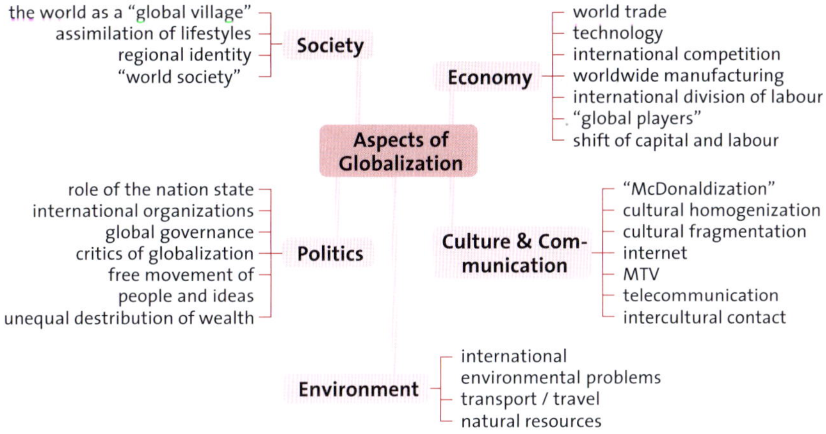

Basics **Globalization**

Globalization can be defined as a "comprehensive term for the emergence of a global society in which economic, political, environmental, and cultural events in one part of the world quickly come to have significance for people in other parts of the world". Globalization is seen as "the result of advances in communication, transportation, and information technologies".

13.6.1 Reasons for globalization

The following developments can be considered to have brought about globalization as we know it today:

- **Technology:** the advances in communication – especially the emergence of the Internet since the early 1990s – brought about many changes. It is now quite possible for many firms to produce a product in many geographically distant places. Without the Internet transnational production would hardly be possible. The same is true for international finance markets where modern communication makes it possible to transfer huge sums within seconds.
- **Transport:** the speed of transport has increased tremendously over the past decades while the costs are only a fraction of what they used to be. These factors also contribute to an ever more globalized economy. The world is about to become both one big market place and one big factory; where something is produced and where something is sold is no longer as important as it used to be.
- **The end of the Cold War:** the downfall of the Soviet Union and the consequent end of the east-west conflict opened up large parts of the world that were previously (almost) inaccessible for "western" industry and commerce. This led to a huge increase in worldwide trade and production.
- **Deregulation of the world economy:** the victory of capitalism over socialism at the beginning of the 1990s resulted in a "liberal" economy with open markets and free trade.

13.6.2 Economic aspects

Globalization is far from being just an economic phenomenon. But is probably in the area of economics where the effects of globalization are most felt.

There has been a tremendous increase in world trade; more and more countries are part of that trade. Worldwide manufacturing is another trend in globalization; it is not unusual for a single product to be produced in many places. Some products are designed, manufactured, packed and assembled in ten different countries before they are sold to the consumer. This is made possible by the very low cost of transport and the fact that particular countries are chosen for their role in the production process: labour-intensive parts of the production will go to countries with low wages while the design will take place in another suitable country.

In this new form of international division of labour the so-called **global players** play an important part. They are multinational corporations with worldwide markets and worldwide production outlets. When DaimlerChrysler still existed, the company manufactured cars in 17 countries on all five continents.

13.6.3 Cultural aspects

The term “McDonaldization” has long been a catchword in the discussion about the effects of globalization. It stands for the process of cultural homogenization. Taking the fact that McDonalds can be found almost anywhere in the world as a starting point it is argued that national and regional cultural identities are getting less important and are replaced by a new “international” identity which is dominated largely by “American” and “western” values.

The main vehicles of spreading this new identity are music, television, movies and the Internet. MTV is a good example: founded in 1981 as an American channel to show mainly music videos, it now has dozens of sister channels all over the world. MTV is generally considered to have an enormous impact on popular culture – especially youth culture – almost everywhere. Just like McDonalds, MTV is also a metaphor for a globalized world.

13.6.4 Other aspects

The huge increase in transport and travel over the past decades as well as the industrialization of previously non-industrialized countries has resulted in new threats to the **environment.** This development has made it very difficult to reduce the emission of carbon dioxide, for example, considered to be the main contributor to the greenhouse effect or global warming. Globalization also leads to the increased use of natural resources like water, soil or oil.

In **politics** the emergence of a global economy dominated by powerful multinational corporations has brought up the question of what the role of individual nation states can be. It questions whether one country or one government can still control the effects globalization has on that country. As the big multinational corporations have long since stopped being and thinking "American" or "German" and consider themselves to be true global players for whom national boundaries are no longer very important, many experts believe that the economy and the finance markets can no longer be controlled by national governments. They argue that only international and supranational organizations like the United Nations, the European Union, the World Bank or the International Monetary Fund can attempt to do this. Some people think that a globalized world needs **global governance.** Global governance has been defined as "the management of global processes in the absence of global government" and as "collective efforts to identify, understand or address worldwide problems that go beyond the capacity of individual states to solve."

Discussion **Arguments for and against globalization**

Pros:

- It increases economic growth and produces greater wealth as well as more goods.
- The free flow of capital makes sure that capital is allocated more efficiently.
- Consumers benefit from a greater freedom of choice and from cheaper products.
- Developing countries are given a chance for development.

Cons:

- Instead of creating more economic and social equality, globalization in fact leads to more inequality as well as to greater poverty and social conflict.
- Ordinary people have very little influence on the process of globalization.
- Economic interests and developments are at the centre of globalization while topics like human rights, ecological and social standards and democracy only play a minor role.
- It is feared that globalization will result in the loss of jobs and lower wages in the richer countries.

14
The English-Speaking World

As a term, the English-speaking world describes those countries where English is an **official** or de facto official or **national** language. Also included are countries where English is an official but not primary language. English is the official language in 53 countries, ranging from the United States with well over 200 million speakers to Malta will less than 500,000 speakers.

English is the official language in the United Kingdom and Australia, for example. In India, English is also an official language but it is not the primary language.

All English-speaking countries have one thing in common: they share historical, political and cultural characteristics rooted in the historical experience of the United Kingdom or the United States. In more practical terms one can say that most English-speaking countries were – at one time in their history – closely connected with Britain or the US, either as **colonies** or **dependencies.** Sometimes the term **Anglosphere** is used to describe **anglophone** nations.

English ranks third in the list of **native** speakers (after Chinese/Mandarin and Spanish) and second in the list of **total** speakers.

English is now the de facto **lingua franca** (world language) because of its large numbers of speakers – both native and non-native – and its use in international organisations and the academic community.

Number of natives speakers by country

Country	Native speakers (approx.)
United States	215 million
United Kingdom	58 million
Philippines	42 million
Canada	18 million
Australia	15 million
Ireland	4 million
South Africa	3.6 million
New Zealand	3.5 million
Jamaica	2.6 million
Singapore	2 million

14.1 Australia

The **Commonwealth of Australia** consists of the world's smallest continent, the island of Tasmania and numerous other islands in the Indian and Pacific Oceans. It has a population of almost 22 million, including 400,000 Aborigines (indigenous population). Australia is a member of the Commonwealth of Nations. Its capital is Canberra, its largest city Sydney. It is a prosperous, technologically advanced and industrialised multicultural country.

History

The Australian continent was first sighted by Europeans at the beginning of the 17th century. However, no attempt was made at settlement. In 1770, James Cook sailed along and mapped the east coast of Australia, which he named New South Wales and claimed for Great Britain. A **penal colony** was later established and roughly 165,000 convicts were transported to the Australian penal colonies by the British government between 1786 and 1868. British colonies were created and settled in Tasmania, South Australia, Victoria and Queensland during the first half of the 19th century. More settlers came to Australia during the gold rush of the 1850s.

The indigenous Australian population **(Aborigines),** estimated at 350,000 at the time of European settlement, declined steeply for 150 years, mainly because of infectious disease.

In 1901 a federation of the colonies was achieved and the Commonwealth of Australia was born as a **dominion** of the British Empire, giving Australia a certain degree of autonomy. Most constitutional links between Australia and the United Kingdom ended between 1942 and 1986. Today Australia is a member of the Commonwealth; Queen Elizabeth II is the Queen of Australia and is represented in Australia by the Governor-General.

Geography and demographics

Australia has six states and two major mainland territories. The states are New South Wales, Queensland, South Australia, Tasmania, Victoria and Western Australia. The major mainland territories are the Northern Territory and the Australian Capital Territory.

By far the largest part of Australia is **desert** or semi-arid lands commonly known as the **outback.** It is the driest inhabited continent; its population density is among the lowest in the world. Its largest cities are Sydney, Melbourne, Brisbane and Perth.

Most Australians are descended from colonial-era settlers and immigrants form Europe. Almost 90 % of the population are of European descent, with the vast majority coming from Britain and Ireland. An ambitious **immigration programme** brought nearly six million immigrants to Australia between 1945 and 2000. The indigenous population is now slightly over 400,000.

Australia: states and mainland territories

Australia today

Australia consistently ranks among the **top 10** countries in the world as far as prosperity, economic performance, life expectancy or quality of life is concerned and remains a multicultural country that is attractive to immigrants. In recent years most immigrants came form Asia and Oceania.

Australia has twice hosted the Olympic Games, in 1956 (Melbourne) and in 2000 (Sydney). Its cities are ranked very high in the world's most liveable cities list, with Melbourne reaching second place. The service industry, including tourism, education and financial services, accounts for almost 70 % of GDP.

14.2 South Africa

The **Republic of South Africa** is located at the southern tip of the African continent. Neighbouring countries are Namibia, Botswana, Zimbabwe and Mozambique. About 48 million people live in South Africa, 80 % of them Black, the others White (9 %), Coloured (9 %) or Asian (2 %). Its capital is Pretoria, its largest city is Johannesburg. South Africa is among the most prosperous countries on the African continent. It has a modern infrastructure and a good supply of natural resources. It also has one of the highest rates of income inequality in the world.

History

European colonization began with Dutch settlers in the second half of the 17th century in the Cape Town area. Britain took over that area in 1806 and encouraged British settlement. During the 1830s, the **Boers** – mainly Dutch settlers trying to escape British rule – departed from the Cape Colony and migrated to the future Natal, Orange Free State und Transvaal regions (known as the Boer Republics).

The 1860s and 1880s saw an increase in immigration to South Africa because diamonds and gold were discovered. There was much conflict over the control of these resources between Europeans and the subjugated indigenous population, and also between the Boers and the British. Two **Boer Wars** were fought between the Boers and the British before and at the turn of the 20th century. Britain finally took control.

In 1910 the Union of South Africa was created from the Cape and Natal colonies, as well as the republics of Orange Free State and Transvaal. The new state was a dominion of Great Britain, giving it some degree of autonomy. The Statute of Westminster effectively granted independence from the United Kingdom in 1931. The country left the Commonwealth in 1961 and became a republic.

Basics **Apartheid**

There had always been **racial segregation** when South Africa was under Dutch and British control. It was intensified, however, when the National Party was elected to power in 1948. The Government systematised existing segregationist laws, classifying all peoples into three races, developing rights and limitations for each, such as pass laws and residential restrictions. The white minority controlled the vastly larger black majority. The system of segregation became known collectively as **apartheid.**

Apartheid became increasingly controversial, leading to widespread sanctions, divestment and growing unrest and oppression. A long period of harsh suppression by the government, and at times violent resistance, strikes, marches, protests, and sabotage by bombing and other means, by various anti-apartheid movements, most notably the **African National Congress (ANC),** followed.

In 1990 the National Party government lifted the ban on the ANC and released **Nelson Mandela** from prison after 27 years. Apartheid legislation was repealed and South Africa held its first multi-racial elections in 1994, which the ANC won by an overwhelming majority. Nelson Mandela was elected as President in May, 1994, and formed a government of national unity. Nelson Mandela and Frederik Willem de Klerk – Mandela's predecessor as State President – received the 1993 **Nobel Peace Price** for their joint efforts to abolish apartheid.

Geography and demographics

The Republic of South Africa consists of nine provinces, including Free State and Western Cape. It has a long coastline across two oceans (the South Atlantic and the Indian). There is considerable variation in climate as well as topography.

The 48 million people living in South Africa are of diverse origins, cultures and languages. The majority of the population classifies itself as **African** or black, but it is not culturally or linguistically homogenous. The same is true for the **white population** which descend from many ethnic groups: Dutch, Portuguese, English and Irish, among others. Culturally and linguistically they are divided into the **Afrikaners** (who speak Afrikaans) and English-speaking groups, many of who are descended from British and Irish immigrants.

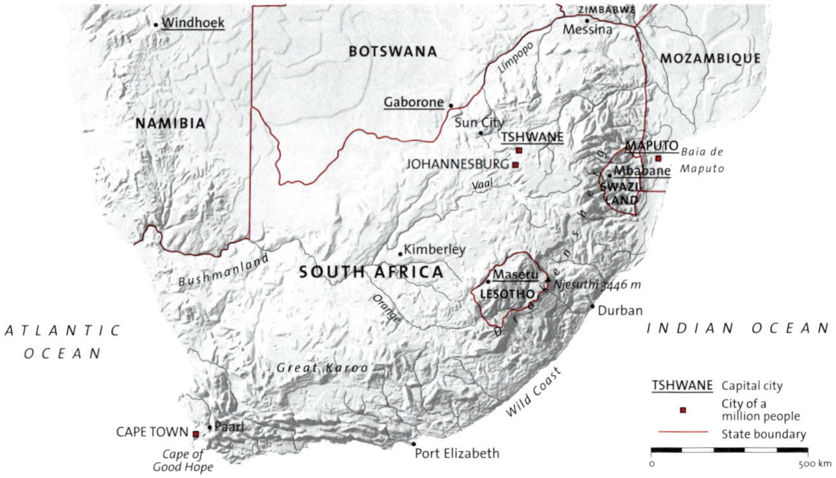

South Africa

South Africa today

Two decades after the end of apartheid South Africa is a country with many problems. Millions of South Africans, mostly black, have continued to live in **poverty.** Poverty among whites, previously rare, has increased greatly. The **crime rate,** especially in the big cities, is very high; this has lead many middle-class South Africans to move into gated communities or even to leave the country. South Africa has also been experiencing a **"brain drain"** with many skilled people leaving the country.

One of the biggest problems is the **HIV/AIDS pandemic.** In 2005 the infection rate among adults was estimated at 20 %. The number of infected pregnant women was even higher with 31 %. Aids is far more prevalent in the black population. The total number of infected people is probably roughly five million out of a total population of 48 million. Most people infected with the HIV virus do not receive sufficient antiretroviral therapy. Many families lose their primary wage earners; this results in a huge number of "AIDS orphans", estimated to be at 1.4 million in 2007.

14.3 Jamaica and the Caribbean

The Caribbean comprises more than **7,000 islands** and reefs in the Caribbean Sea southeast of the Gulf of Mexico. These islands are called the **West Indies** (because Columbus believed that he had reached the Indies). Among the better known islands are the **Bahamas, Barbados, Cuba, Jamaica** and **Trinidad and Tobago.** The total population of the region was estimated to be at 37.5 million in 2000. While there is a strong Spanish influence in the Caribbean (countries like Cuba and the Dominican Republic are Spanish-speaking countries), English is an official language in most countries of the region.

History

All islands in the Caribbean were at some point colonies of European nations. The **British West Indies** (Antigua and Barbuda, Bahamas, Barbados, British Virgin Islands, Cayman Islands, Grenada, Jamaica, Trinidad and Tobago amongst others) were colonized by the British in the 17th century. A **plantation system** was introduced where slaves were forced to work on sugar plantations. **Sugar** was Britain's largest import by the middle of the 18th century, showing the importance of the Caribbean colonies.

Slavery was abolished in the 19th century, but this did not really improve the situation of the indigenous people. Wages were extremely low, sugar production and trade was controlled by the colonizing nations. Countries in the Caribbean continued to be dependent on the plantation system, with little or no capital to invest in other areas like industry. Most countries stayed poor even after they became politically independent in the 19th or 20th century.

Islands in and near the Caribbean

Geography and demographics

The geography and climate in the Caribbean region varies from one place to another. Some islands in the region have relatively flat terrain of non-volcanic origin. Others possess rugged towering mountain-ranges. The climate of the region is tropical and hurricanes often hit the area.

If one takes **Jamaica** as an example one will discover that over 90 % of the population are of **African** descent and about 6 % have a **multiracial** background. The official language is English, but **Jamaican Patois** is more commonly spoken by a majority of the population. It is considered to be an English dialect and has its root in 17th-century English and African languages as well as some European languages.

Jamaica has a population of 2.8 million. This makes it the third most populous anglophone country in North America, after the United States and Canada. Its capital and largest city is Kingston. About one third of the island's population live in the Kingston metropolitan area and about half live in urban areas.

Jamaica today

Major sectors of the Jamaican economy include agriculture (raw sugar), mining (bauxite, alumina), manufacturing (garment industry), tourism and finance. Tourism is of particular importance since it is Jamaica's main source of foreign exchange and information technologies are of growing importance for its economy.

The **Rastafari** movement had a strong influence on Jamaica. This Back to Africa movement believes that Haile Selassie of Ethiopia was God incarnate, the returned black messiah, come to take the lost Twelve Tribes of Israel back to live with him in Holy Mount Zion in a world of perfect peace, love and harmony. **Bob Marley,** a convert to the faith, spread the message of Rastafari to the world. There are now estimated to be more than a million Rastafarians throughout the world. Jamaica's music – **reggae** for example – has a global presence.

14.4 India

The **Republic of India** on the Indian subcontinent is the second-most populous country and the most populous democracy in the world. It has a total population of 1.15 billion (2008 estimate). India consists of 28 states and seven union territories. Its capital is New Delhi; its largest city is Mumbai (formerly Bombay). India is one of the fastest growing economies in the world and ranks among the world's top 15 economies (GDP). Despite of this India still remains one of the poorest countries in the world, with 42 % of the population living below the international poverty line. Hindi and English are official languages.

India

History

European colonization of India started in the 16th century. By 1865 most of India was under the control of the **British East India Company.** One year later India was brought under the direct rule of the British Crown. The period of British rule between 1858 and 1947 is referred to as the **British Raj.**

The second part of the 19th century saw major changes in India: Railways, roads, canals, and bridges were rapidly built and telegraph links equally rapidly established so that raw materials, such as cotton, from India's hinterland could be transported more efficiently to ports, such as Bombay, for subsequent export to England. Likewise, finished goods from England were transported back just as efficiently, for sale in the burgeoning Indian markets.

Trade between Britain and India was **"unequal":** Instead of using the country's raw materials like cotton to build up a textile industry in India, the cotton was bought for a cheap price and was shipped to Britain where textiles were made in British factories. These textiles were then shipped to India, among other places, and sold for a high price. As a result of all this there was economic progress in Britain, but no or next to no development in India. **Jawaharlal Nehru,** India's first prime minister, argued that "those parts of India which have been longest under British rule are the poorest today".

In 1935, the British Parliament approved the **Government of India Act,** which authorised the establishment of independent legislative assemblies in all provinces of British India and the creation of a central government. In 1947, Britain decided to end British rule of India and announced its intention of transferring power no later than 1948. The country was partitioned along religious lines. The predominantly Hindu and Sikh areas were assigned to the new **India** and predominantly Muslim areas to the new nation of **Pakistan.**

Biography **Mahatma Gandhi (1869–1948)**

Mahatma Gandhi (Mohandas Karamchand Gandhi) was the most important political and spiritual leader of the Indian independence movement. He is officially honoured in India as the **Father of the Nation,** he is also called Bapu (father) in India.

As a young man, Gandhi experienced discrimination directed at Indians in South Africa, where he worked as a lawyer for an Indian firm. He took part in the resident Indian community's struggle for civil rights and first employed non-violent **civil disobedience** there.

He became the leader of the **Indian National Congress** (a party) in 1921 and employed **non-cooperation, non-violence** and **peaceful resistance** as his "weapons" in the struggle against the British in India. He remained the leader of the Indian National Congress during the period of the partitioning of the country and its independence from Britain. He was assassinated on January 30, 1948 by a Hindu radical.

Geography and demographics

India is a culturally, linguistically and genetically diverse geographical unit. It is home to two major linguistic families: Indo-Aryan (Hindi, Urdu) and Dravidian (Tamil, Telugu, Kannada). **Hindi** has the largest number of speakers and is the official language. **English,** which is extensively used in business and administration, has the status of "subsidiary official language" and is also important in education.

Over 800 million Indians out of a total of 1.15 billion are **Hindu.** Other religious groups include **Muslims, Christians** and **Sikhs.** India has the highest population of Muslims for a non-Muslim majority country.

Traditional Indian society is defined by relatively strict **social hierarchy.** The Indian **caste system** describes the social stratification and social restrictions on the Indian subcontinent, in which social classes are defined by thousands of hereditary groups, often termed as castes, where having close personal relationships or marrying outside the group is not customary. Arranged marriages are still common for a majority of Indians.

India today

India's **economy** is among the fastest growing in the world. It has the world's second largest labour force. The service sector is by far the largest sector, with agriculture ranking second and industry third (GDP by sector). The Indian economy is expected to grow even further and might surpass the United States before 2050. Economic inequality has widened with India's recent economic growth and is expected to widen even further.

India has one of the world's fastest growing **car industries.** Tata Motors (Mumbai) bought Jaguar and Land Rover from Ford in 2008 and has started to produce the world's cheapest motor car, the Nano.

Information technology is among the fastest growing sectors in India. One the one hand there is a large pool of low cost, but highly skilled, educated and fluent English-speaking workers in India, on the other hand there is an increased demand from European and American businesses to **outsource** their operations. Many call centres are operated in India and many well-known software and IT-firms use the competence of Indian programmers and software engineers. Many firms are placed in **Bangalore,** the Silicon Valley of India.

Basics **India's Silicon Valley**

The Silicon Valley of India is a nickname for the city of Bangalore, India's third most populous city. It is a hub for **information technology companies** that specialise in research and development, electronics and software production. Foreign companies based in Bangalore include Adobe, Amazon, AMD, Bosch, Cisco, Dell, Google, Intel, Microsoft and Siemens.

Extra: Vocabulary Landeskunde

Politics	
accountable	verantwortlich
acquittal	Freispruch
advocate	Befürworter
anachronism	Zustand, der nicht mehr zeitgemäß ist
appellate court	Berufungsgericht
assembly	Regionalparlament
bicameral system	Zwei-Kammer-System
branch of government	Zweig/Teil der Staatsorgane
budget	Etat (eines Staates)
checks and balances	*Gewaltenteilung in den USA; gegenseitige Kontrolle*
collective responsibility	gemeinsame Verantwortung
common law	Gewohnheitsrecht
consent	Zustimmung
constituency	Wahlkreis
constitutional monarchy	konstitutionelle Monarchie
contested	umstritten
court of appeal	Berufungsgericht
devolution	Dezentralisierung, Regionalisierung
elector	Wahlmann
federal government	Bundesregierung
first-past-the-post system	Mehrheitswahlrecht
general election	Parlamentswahlen
hereditary peer	*Mitglied des Oberhauses mit erblichem Titel*
impeachment	Amtsenthebungsklage
judiciary	Judikative, richterliche Gewalt
life peer	*Mitglied des Oberhauses auf Lebenszeit*
majority vote	Mehrheitsbeschluss
MP (Member of Parliament)	Abgeordneter
partisan	parteiisch, einer Partei folgend
poll	Meinungsumfrage
popular vote	Wählerstimmen
premature	vorzeitig
prerogative	Vorrecht
proportional representation	Verhältniswahl
ratification, to ratify	Ratifizierung (eines Vertrages), ratifizieren
redistribution	Umverteilung
remnant	Überbleibsel
single currency	einheitliche Währung
stance	Einstellung, Haltung
term	Wahlperiode, Amtszeit
to appoint	ernennen
to dissolve	auflösen
to enact	gesetzlich verfügen
to overthrow	stürzen, zu Fall bringen
to rectify	berichtigen
to step down	zurücktreten

trade union	Gewerkschaft
unalienable	unveräußerlich
unconditional	bedingungslos
unitary state	Einheitsstaat, Zentralstaat
vote of no confidence	Misstrauensvortum
whip	Fraktionseinpeitscher

Economy

bad debt	„schlechte“ Schulden/Wertpapiere
boom	Wirtschaftsaufschwung
competitive	wettbewerbsfähig
decline	Niedergang
deficit	Fehlbetrag, Schulden
demand	Nachfrage
devaluation	Abwertung (einer Währung)
economic sector	Sektor/Bereich einer Volkswirtschaft
enterprise	Unternehmen, Unternehmungsgeist
entrepreneurial	unternehmerisch
expansion	Ausdehnung
GDP (gross domestic product)	Bruttoinlandsprodukt (BIP)
greed	Geldgier
growth	Wachstum
innovation	Neuerung
laissez-faire	wirtschaftsliberales Verhalten
mobility	Mobilität
monetarism	Monetarismus, Geldwirtschaft
nationalisation	Verstaatlichung
post-industrial	postindustriell (nach dem industriellen Zeitalter)
privatisation	Privatisierung
public spending	öffentliche Ausgaben, Staatsausgaben
quaternary sector	quartärer Sektor (Informationsdienstleistungen)
resources	Mittel, Rohstoffquellen
socioeconomic	sozialwirtschaftlich
stagnation	Flaute, Stagnation
strife	Streit, Auseinandersetzung
supply	Angebot
sustained	auf Dauer angelegt
taxation	Besteuerung
to fluctuate	schwanken; steigen und fallen
trade union	Gewerkschaft
work ethic	Arbeitsethos, Arbeitsmoral

Social Issues

(social) class	Schicht, Klasse
abolitionism	Bewegung zur Abschaffung der Sklaverei
allowances	finanzielle Hilfe, Beihilfe
assimilation	Anpassung
benefits	Sozialleistungen, Zuwendungen

blue collar	Arbeiter
civil disobedience	ziviler Ungehorsam
class distinction	Klassenunterschied
class-consciousness	Klassenbewusstsein
classification	Einordnung
clerical	Büro …
demographic	bevölkerungsstatistisch, -wissenschaftlich
distribution	Verteilung
egalitarian	egalitär, gleichmacherisch
ethnicity	Zugehörigkeit zu einer ethnischen Gruppe
executive	Regierung
harassment	Belastigung, Schikane
hazard	Gefahr
indigenous	eingeboren, einheimisch
influx	Zustrom
managerial	führend
mandatory	gesetzlich vorgeschrieben
mean income	statistisches Durchschnittseinkommen
mutual	gegenseitig, wechselseitig, einvernehmlich
poverty line	Armutsgrenze
poverty rate	Armutsquote
professional	Berufstätiger mit qualifizierter Ausbildung
segregation	Rassentrennung
self-reliance	Eigenständigkeit
skilled	ausgebildet, qualifiziert
social division	soziale Spaltung
social grade	soziale Rangstufe
social mobility	soziale Mobilität
social values	gesellschaftliche Werte
stratification	soziale Schichtung
undocumented person	Ausländer ohne notwendige Papiere
Welfare State	Wahlfahrtsstaat, Sozialstaat
white collar	Angesteller

Education

(academic) prerequisite	(Grund-) Voraussetzung (bezüglich der Ausbildung)
academic standards	Ausbildungsniveau
achievement	Leistung
assembly	Schulversammlung
compulsory education	Schulpflicht
elective course	Wahlkurs
extra-curricular	außerhalb des Lehrplans
fee-paying	Schulgeld
grade	Klasse
graduate	Schulabgänger, Universitätsabsolvent
graduation	Abschlussfeier
home schooling	Privatunterricht zuhause, Hausunterricht

K-12	*Kürzel für das amerikanische Schulsystem*
public school	Privatschule (in GB)
schedule	Stundenplan
scholarship	Stipendium
school board	lokale Schulbehörde
term	Schuljahresabschnitt, „Halbjahr“
truancy	Schuleschwänzen

Mass Media	
broadcasting	Rundfunk/Fernsehen
broadsheet	großformatige Zeitung
fractured	zersplittert
investigative journalism	Enthüllungsjournalismus
prime time	Haupteinschaltzeit
soap	Seifenoper
subscription TV	Bezahlfernsehen
syndication	Veröffentlichung in versch. Zeitungen/Ausstrahlung auf versch. TV-Stationen
tabloid	kleinformatige Zeitung
terrestrial TV	terrestrisches Fernsehen

International Relations	
anglophone	englischsprachig
bipolar	zweipolig
credibility gap	Glaubwürdigkeitslücke
crime rate	Kriminalitätsrate
decolonisation	Entkolonialisierung
deregulation	Liberalisierung, Deregulierung
dominion	Dominion, Herrschaftsgebiet
expansion	Ausdehnung
global governance	weltweite Steuerung durch die Politik
hegemony	Vorherrschaft
homogenization	Vereinheitlichung
isolationism	Isolationspolitik
labour force	Erwerbsbevökerung
legacy	Erbe, Hinterlassenschaft
pandemic	Epidemie, die einen großen Teil eines Landes betrifft
Patois	Dialekt des Englischen in Jamaica
penal colony	Strafkolonie
plantation	Plantage
power sharing	Teilung der politischen Macht
preventive war	vorbeugender Krieg, Präventivkrieg
prodominantly	überwiegend
resistance	Widerstand
to outsource	ausgliedern, auslagern
to partition	teilen
unilateral	einseitig
weapons decommissioning	Abgabe von Waffen

Register